THE VENDING INDUSTRY

HISTORY
TRENDS
SECRETS
OPPORTUNITIES
SCAMS

BY

CHARLES HANNA

Copyright © 1979
Charles Hanna

All rights reserved. No part of this book may be reproduced in any form without permission in writing from the author or publisher.

Second Printing: October 2001

Library of Congress Catloging-in-Publication Data
Hanna, Charles A. (Charles Anthony)

The Vending Industry: History, Trends, Secrets, Opportunities, and Scams / Charles A. Hanna.

ISBN 978-0-9714930-8-7

1. Vending   2. Vending Equipment   3. Vending Machines

Chapter 5 photography provided by Tiffany Hanna.
Book and cover design by Selma Steinhilber.

For information on how you may purchase additional copies of this book for delivery by mail or for quantity purchases, please contact:
The Hanna Group
913-894-4979
Charles@hanna-vending.com

Printed in the United States by Morris Publishing
3212 East Highway 30
Kearney, NE 68847
1-800-650-7888

Mission Statement

We will remain the diversified vending industry leader by humbly working with the very smallest prospect, customer or creditor as we would the largest opportunity in the world....with great respect, integrity, honesty, fairness and patience.....

We will promise the moon but deliver the stars whenever possible, due to our ongoing, hardworking, yet smart thinking, innovative and dedicated team effort..

Finally....The Book On Vending that will Totally Educate You!

THE VENDING INDUSTRY
* History * Opportunities * Secrets * Trends *Scams.
by Charles Hanna

A 26 year veteran of the vending industry and owner of Hanna Vending, Charles Hanna decided that it was time to present the history, secrets, trends, opportunities and scams for the general public, the vending industry and especially for entrepreneurs who have an attraction for the world of vending. Hanna also published; The World's First Vending Machine Price Catalog which remains the one and only 52 page color vending machine price catalog in the vending industry!

You will learn in this book about how to start a vending business and detect scams and also have a better appreciation for the tremendous variety and types of vending machines and vending services being offered in the market.

You will learn about the twelve commandments of vending, product and equipment supplies, public relations, equipment depreciation, accounting, and tax tips.

Hanna shares details on how to get new locations and implement marketing and sales strategies that he used in his multi-million dollar vending business which he started from one vending machine in 1976.

He covers important strategies such as financing and how to get it! Hanna gives insight as to how much to pay for a vending business and all the pros and cons of working for an established vending company versus owning your own vending company and much, much more.

Get your hands on this book if you have any interest in the vending industry or if you are already in vending and just need to sharpen your skills. Why not learn directly from the man who has done it all successfully?

TO ORDER ADDITIONAL COPIES OF THIS BOOK CONTACT:
The Hanna Group
P.O. Box 14304-4304
Lenexa, KS 66215
Tel: 913-894-4979
Fax: 913-894-0252
Charles@hanna-vending.com
http://www.hanna-vending.com

ACKNOWLEDGEMENTS

I would like to take this opportunity to thank some very special people who helped and influenced me in many ways over the years in my business and also with my book.

My parents, Habib and Victoria Hanna who taught me everything I know about business. I cannot begin to express my love and appreciation for being so fortunate to learn from them first hand. They heard me talk about writing this book for many years and enthusiastically encouraged me to do so. One of my regrets in life is that they never lived to see it to completion.

My family members (Linda, Tiffany & Krystal) who have tolerated my strong passion for business and somehow managed during the rough times and the countless long days and nights that I was away at the office.

My brothers Rene, Joe, and Michael and my sister, Janet for sharing their strengths with me.

Dick Roughton, my dear friend who believed in me even when all the odds were against me and I doubted myself.

Binney Orlich and her mother Virginia George, who influenced my decision to leave Jamaica and come to America after the loss of my family's business and the loss of my music career.

My late father-in-law Andre Abrajano and my mother-in-law Peggy for being so sweet and loving toward me.

I would also like to thank both my old and new friends who have been encouraging over the years and have always been ready, willing and able to take time out to be true friends. Eric and Pearl Dunkley, Sue Coffel, Armen Yousseffi, and Jeff

Duce. Thanks to Naomi Orenczak and Jeanne Heisler and also Katie Jones who provided valuable input regarding graphic design and related matters. I want to acknowledge all my customers, creditors, business associates, friends, family and others who have been encouraging me for the past 25 years to write this book.

I cannot possibly mention every one of the precious individuals who helped me with the various aspects of growing my business and writing this book. Finally, special thanks to Selma Steinhilber who helped me pull several aspects of the book together and designed my new corporate logo.

TESTIMONIALS

"Like the Hanna Group used our services, we encourage small businesses to take advantage of our many excellent resources the SBA has to offer. Simply put, our mission is to help small businesses succeed."

Barbara Caldwell
SBA, Public Information Officer

"Charles Hanna is at the cutting edge of the continually evolving vending industry. He offers a helping hand and takes keen interest in educating and counseling individuals and corporations both nationally and internationally with regard to vending and related matters."

Michael Hoffman
President, Hoffman Mint

"Charles Hanna was extremely helpful and supportive from the very beginning and his management and staff continue to help in our successful growth."

Ben L. Cleveland
C&C Vending

"Charles has devoted countless hours to building his vending company successfully just as he has done for the Lenexa Chamber of Commerce. He was designated Member of the Year, "Lifetime Member, People's Choice Award and Chamber Member of the Year (for recruiting most new members). He has continued serving the Chamber for many years through tireless service on many action committees and the Board of Directors."

Colonel Frank Weimer, USAF (Ret.) & former Executive Director of the Lenexa Chamber of Commerce

"Charles Hanna continues to think outside of the box and helps individuals get started in our industry on the right foot. For many years he has featured only quality vending and related equipment in his World's First Vending Machine Price Catalog. This new book he has recently released on the vending industry should be of continued significant benefit to all who desire learning more about vending and "buying in" at an honest/fair price point."

Ron Barnes
Dixie-Narco, NE

"We have been extremely pleased to have been associated with Charles Hanna and his fine organization for more than twelve years. Always an astute businessman, Charles clearly understands that ensuring complete customer satisfaction yields repeat business and long term growth for his organization and ours. His impressive knowledge of this industry and its unique characteristics is crucial in helping his customers make the right purchasing decisions."

Bill Kreitz
CEO, Savamco Manufacturing, Inc.

As a friend and a vending client for twenty-five years, I am pleased that Charles Hanna will now formally share his vending expertise with the rest of the world. All readers and decision makers will benefit from his integrity, broad international and national business acumen and personal humanitarian nature in this regard."

Craig May
President
Auto Jalisco
Indiana

"Beware of advertisements that offer unrealistic returns. If it looks too good to be true....it probably is. Charles Hanna shares these concerns and is doing something positive to prevent such scams."

David F. Essay
Pepsi-Cola Bottling, NE

TABLE OF CONTENTS

HISTORY OF VENDING	1
HOW TO START A VENDING BUSINESS AND DETECT SCAMS	11
TYPES OF VENDING MACHINES	19
TYPES OF VENDING SERVICES	27
TWELVE COMMANDMENTS OF VENDING	31
PRODUCT AND EQUIPMENT SUPPLY	48
MORE ON SCAMS	56
PUBLIC RELATIONS	66
EQUIPMENT DEPRECIATION, ACCOUNTING AND TAX TIPS	72
HOW TO GET NEW LOCATIONS ...MARKETING AND SALES	78
YOU ARE INVITED TO MEET THE MANAGER..... NOW WHAT?	91
FINANCING ....HOW WILL YOU GET IT?	101
HOW MUCH SHOULD YOU PAY FOR A VENDING BUSINESS	111
WORKING FOR AN EXISTING VENDING COMPANY	119

SOME IMPORTANT TRAITS TO REMEMBER	132
CONCLUSION	139
PHOTO GALLERY	141
ABOUT THE AUTHOR	145

Chapter 1
THE HISTORY OF VENDING

For thousands of years people have been fascinated by the possibilities and uniqueness of an "automatic cash up front" type of business. Many enjoy the concept of making money by selling items, collecting for it, dispensing the item, yet never meeting the customer! When I was a little boy, I used to buy a cup of soda from a vending machine at school in Kingston, Jamaica for six pence (British money).... What a thrill!

Some time later, while I was a student in Beirut, Lebanon I would pay 25 Piasters (Lebanese money) for a small bottle of Coca-Cola from a small vending machine. It was a wonder to me how the machine could figure out how to charge the right amount every time! I often wondered how the vending machine knew the difference between coins and values in the various countries of the world? While standing in line to buy a product from the vending machine, my friends and I anticipated the thrill of the automatic response that we would receive once money was inserted and the appropriate button pushed. I thought that the vending machine was a new invention and that I was a lucky space age kid who was among the very first to learn about this phenomenon!

It is interesting to think back to what it must have been like to live in the days of the Roman Empire, ancient Egypt and the great empires of times gone by. These magnificent traders such as the Phoenicians must have wondered what it would have been like to pick up buckets full of gold nuggets in small self-contained dispensing units that would not need an attendant!

When first beginning the vending business, I started to make notes of the historic moments in the world of vending. I wrote down questions, and accumulated tidbits, which I often included in my Hanna Newsletters. I often found it insurmountable gather all the fascinating details about an industry with which I had fallen in love. I spoke with hundreds of vending machine operators, manufacturers, product suppliers and a wide variety of related industry leaders and "old timers" who gladly shared incredible details with me.

In this chapter you will learn about some of the history of vending. I hope you will find this information very interesting and thought provoking, regardless of your personal or business background.

215 B.C.
The mathematician Hero produced a book entitled PNEUMATICA describing many of his inventions. Many efforts to find the original manuscript had failed and were believed to be lost. However, in 1587 a copy of that original manuscript was discovered. It showed illustrations of a coin-actuated device, which was to be used for vending sacrificial water in Egyptian temples. The heavy coin would drop onto lever type devise. This would cause a cork to be pulled out of a custom built spigot with the precise timing to release a small trickle of holy water to the customer! Imagine how exciting it would have been to attempt implementing any such creation in those times.

50 B.C.
In ancient Rome, one man who operated a public bath (Health club) solved the manpower problem with the "honor system." The customer dropped his coin in a wooden box located by the entrance to the bath. No one bothered the money once it was in the box, because of the poisonous snakes resting in the bottom with the coins! Many believe that this may have been the earliest record of "unattended" or "automated merchandising." Such brilliance! This strategy would also probably

work even in today's marketplace!

1076 A.D.
Chinese brilliance and imagination was the engine behind a coin-operated pencil machine. Why am I not surprised? The Chinese have always been known for "Sharpening their pencils" and they have proven over and over how they can effectively and successfully compete in the world market! I had thought that it was only since I was growing up in modern times that the Chinese were so creative, however, it appears to me that some things never change!

1700's
During this era, coin-operated Tobacco Boxes were reported to make their first appearance in English taverns. The tobacco industry of those days may possibly have had the same powerful influence on their customers. Creating similar ingenious marketing techniques added new ways to increase sales.

1880's - Vending in the USA
As far as we can determine, several patents for coin-operated dispensers were granted in the U.S. during this time. Tutti-Frutti gum machines were installed in New York near the train stations. The Thomas Adams Company created these. Other machine type dispensers appeared in Utah in the 1890's. Crude as they were, you could get a divorce decree or a marriage license with just a silver dollar! What a concept! When I learned about a company in the USA in the mid 1990's who were introducing a vending machine for divorce documents, I thought they had an original idea! Not!

1902
We were introduced to the first completely coin operated restaurant, Horn & Hardart, which opened in Philadelphia. The operation actually survived until the 1960's when they

were forced to close down due to the rapid growth of the fast food chains that had began to spread across the USA and the world.

1905
U.S. Post Office investigates use of stamp machines and actually implemented their use. Until today, they continue to be successful. They are further investigating all sorts of new ways to make current and collectable stamps and related items even more accessible to the American public via this incredible outlet known to us as "Stamp vending merchandisers".

1930's
It was soon after the introduction of cigarette vending machines in the 1920's that vending began to be noticed a little more. However, it was really not until the 1930's that the vending machine concept or "automatic merchandising" as we call it today, was introduced. It created quite an impression in some cities, when for only a penny, your favorite gum or candy could be purchased automatically! Most important, machines featuring familiar bottled soft drinks, cooled with ice, appeared on the market. With all the new activity going on, the National Automatic Merchandising Association was founded in 1936.

1940's
Though the world sadly mourned during the 1940's and WW II, the shortage of manpower and womanpower and the need for around-the-clock snack service in defense plants meant a real expansion in the use of vending machines. It led the way for the rapid spread of "on location" vending in offices, factories, hospitals, etc. Total sales of vended products soon reached $600 million. It was during this era that the first coffee vending machines were introduced. This gave a new meaning to the term, "coffee break". This is still one of the most popular business phrases we use to refer to "time out" in the new millennia!

1950's.
The so-called "Baby Boom" after WW II, resulted in a population explosion in the 1950's. More people everywhere recognized the need for more vending machines. It was at this time the industry began to fall behind, as a whole. The first refrigerated sandwich vending machine expanded what was to become the first automated lunch menu. The U.S. Public Health Service approved the Model Vending Sanitation Code. Mergers and acquisitions began to produce several new national vending service firms. If I knew then what I know now, I would have bought stock in the king of colas and the major players among vending machine manufacturers and service organizations during those times. It must have been very exciting to be in the middle of such a booming industry. Many common American coins were still made of silver during this time! Too bad I was only a young boy with no idea of the automated revolution in motion.

1960's
By the time the 60's era rolled around, the demand for luxury, convenience and superior service had reached another all time high. There was even more demand for "automated merchandising" which was still not fully realized. The busier people became, the more services they demanded. It seemed as if everyone wanted everything yesterday! Cup and canned soft drink vending machines appeared on the scene everywhere. Dollar changers and microwave ovens were soon introduced. If only I had bought the appropriate vending machine stocks from the 1950 's I would have been ready to possibly retire by the late 1960's! However, it was not yet my time! I would have to be patient till I discovered the world of vending many years later!

1970's & 80's
HANNA INTRODUCES THEIR STYLE OF VENDING:
The Hanna Company Inc. was formed in the early to mid 70's

in Overland Park, Kansas. The company experienced a very humble beginning. I had only recently arrived in America and was followed shortly thereafter by my younger brother Michael and other members of our family who were all new immigrants to America. Our family had lost most of our assets over seas due to political and unstable problems in Jamaica where I was born and raised. Later we lost more of our substantial assets in Beirut, Lebanon, which is our country of origin. In Lebanon, we lost most of our assets due to the Lebanese civil war that was to last more than 20 years! We escaped from total devastation of bombs, murder, kidnapping, looting and gratefully stepped into the land of opportunity and made America our final home.

HOW I STARTED IN THE VENDING BUSINESS:
I was sitting by the swimming pool with a group of friends, at the apartment complex where I lived. I was inquiring about any available jobs in the area or what else I could do to generate some money quickly. Back in those days I had just escaped from the war in Beirut and was trying to temporarily forget my sorrows by having a few drinks with my friends at the swimming pool, which was a few hundred yards from my apartment.

One of my friends mentioned that we were out of potato chips and how nice it would be if someone would volunteer to buy some chips for us to continue enjoying our drinks by the pool. There was no such convenience in the clubhouse and therefore one of us would have to go to the supermarket to buy the chips. Another friend suggested that if only someone would place a potato chip vending machine in the clubhouse that person would become rich! Being the gullible new immigrant that I was, I immediately became intrigued by the comment; and after some more small talk, I gathered the courage to walk straight into the manager's office (While still wearing my bathing suit) and asked if I would be able to place a much needed potato chip vending machine in the club house for the tenants.

I was totally unprepared for the immediate confirmation that I received! I was broke, frightened and desperate to earn a living and could hardly believe my ears when the manager asked me how soon I could have the vending machine installed. Up to that point, I had not been familiar with vending machines...but, at that very moment, my Hanna vending company was born! The rest is history. Our company went on to become a multi-million dollar corporation within the first three to five years of business and we began to diversify into different fields of vending and related operations.

During this interval, the automatic vending industry was bracing itself for the most phenomenal expansion of all time. Less than 1% of all retailing was automatic. The public was being conditioned to vending machines, as never before. Consumers had become far less tolerant of insolent and sloppy sales clerks. Consumers were impatient to go much of a distance to purchase the most basic snack or beverage item during their break or while traveling. They were delightfully discovering that more and more products and services were rapidly becoming available via conveniently placed vending machines. This style of merchandising was greeted with open arms. The vending industry sales volume topped ten billion dollars!

There would be no slowing down of the monster that was created, loved and nourished by the masses. The people welcomed the automatic changes that had become a new way of life. This change was happening, not only with Americans but also with people all over the world.

By 1984, vending product sales topped $16 billion. I was in the right place at the right time. It was hard to imagine that the industry could grow any bigger or more successful than it had since I discovered vending. The growth of Hanna was tremendous in such a short period of time. I felt like a kid in a candy kingdom! It continued to grow substantially. We have expanded over seventeen times in a span of twenty-five years!

The vending industry in the USA was celebrating its 100th anniversary and by the mid 80's credit card and debit card technology was being introduced for the first time in vending machines.

By the time the 90's rolled around, most vending machines had become even more elaborate. Coffee machines were available with choices of cappuccino, espresso, flavored coffees and other hot beverage choices for every taste. The first remote, wireless transmission technology was implemented in vending machines. This made them capable of automatic communication with the vending company's warehouse and office facilities via such new and exciting remote capabilities. Soon thereafter, the new Sacagawea Dollar Gold coin was introduced by the U.S. Mint, which would prove to be most successful. It features the Shoshone Indian Sacagawea. Ironically, the picture on the dollar coin is not really a picture of Sacagawea, for the simple reason that no known likeness exists of her.

2000 & BEYOND

Vending product sales have been in the $25 billion to $30 billion range in the 1990's. A person can get a hot meal, or a cold beer. They can obtain a loan, buy insurance, and purchase a diamond ring and frozen products from vending machines. A customer may use a $1 $2 $5 $10 $20 or larger bill. They might also use dollar coins, or even charge cards and debit cards or remote control devices in automated dispensing equipment. So far, we have only scratched the surface. It would stagger the most liberal imagination to know of the thousands of new and creative ways to market new products and old favorites through "automatic merchandisers". Can you imagine, self-service, coin operated supermarkets or franchised coin operated fast food operations? These are no longer far-fetched dreams.

Countries all over the world offer vending machines of some type or another and yet, there are many countries where vending machines have still not been introduced! The opportunities are endless. I have received numerous phone calls from foreigners internationally, requesting information about opportunities in vending. It is often frustrating to attempt to counsel such individuals who call because they are in essence just starting out from humble beginnings and have no idea of the tremendous head start the rest of the world has had on them! Therefore my company decided that it was time to publish "The World's First Vending Machine Price Catalog". The catalog would help entrepreneurs interested in vending to fully understand the range and availability of the types of vending machines and related equipment. They would also be able to immediately learn about the details of such machines. Most important, new and established vendors could easily learn the factory direct prices at which we would wholesale and ship vending and related equipment and therefore help prevent vending scams.

NOTES

Chapter Two
HOW TO START A VENDING BUSINESS AND DETECT SCAMS!

There are several ways to start a vending business.

Here are some of the most popular ways:

- Business opportunity shows
- Business opportunity classified advertising
- Buying out existing vending companies
- Buying one or two vending machines from individuals
- Buying from vending distributors
- Using locating companies

There are significant drawbacks to getting started if you are not prepared. Numerous scams are operating on large or small-scale basis all over the country of which the potential investor should be aware.

BUSINESS OPPORTUNITY TRADE SHOWS

These shows may well be legitimate in many cases. However the management and sponsors of these shows hardly accept much responsibility for what is being represented. They are not usually or overly concerned to any significant degree regarding the credibility of the individual exhibitor, the equipment they sell or even if you ever receive any of the equipment or services, which were offered. It is strictly a matter of...*let the buyer beware.* I would like to mentioin that the management of most business opportunity trade shows are usually credible individuals but they are not liable for the quality of the exhibitors. Many of the exhibitors are very organized, professional, high-powered and high-pressure sales organizations promising to make you rich overnight! Vending scam artists will promise to sell you a certain number of vending machines, arrange the placement of the equipment, guarantee the results and train you thoroughly for success. Cash up front is always demanded before anything happens. The sales representatives are always very smooth and comprehensive with their sales pitch. Once they have concluded their spiel, which may include brandishing fictitious national statistics, success stories, and cheap talk about exclusive territories, you will be begging to sign on the dotted line and relinquish your cash or cashier's check.

There was a time when I would have been tempted with similar presentations too, however I was broke when I first arrived in America and was unable to spend what I did not have. I thank God for that!

**BUSINESS OPPORTUNITY
CLASSIFIED ADVERTISING**

This method of introducing you to the vending industry is less personal but just as dangerous. This too has the potential capability of separating you from your hard-earned money in a hurry. In most cases, you are interacting with fast-talking and very effective sales specialists. They will attempt to sell you, without delay. They may gather a few dozen unsuspecting potential victims to a local hotel meeting room for a "get rich quick" introduction, presentation and demonstration of the actual vending machines.

In some circumstances, these fast talkers may even offer to fly you into another city and pick you up in a limo to wine and dine you (usually with your own money) then use high pressure sales techniques to close the deal. When you are bundled together with several other potential vending start-ups, they will use some of their own sales people (posing as potential buyers) whom they would have planted at the meeting to make things flow smoother.

They perform a wonderful "dog and pony" show, then move in for a "slam dunk" when they have efficiently overcome all your objections. In many cases they have been known to intimidate those who may ask significant and meaningful questions or have plausible concerns. The sales person will remind you that "they" are the professionals and you should not be concerned whatsoever.

This game moves from city to city with promises of limited exclusive territories, if you act immediately! Heaven forbid you should miss this "once in a life time" opportunity! They will share charts, graphs, statistics, references and a host of classic sales artillery. They will display them in all their majesty to convince you that NOW is the time to buy. They will have you believing that you are in the right place to make the "right decision" and that you should swiftly pull out your checkbook, before they select someone else!

At these demonstrations there are usually a limited line of what would ordinarily be considered by professional vendors to be inferior vending and related equipment on display. Obviously, the prices being quoted are often substantially inflated when compared to the regular selling prices of legitimate companies or when compared to prices listed in our "World's First Vending Machine Price Catalog".

It is surprising to learn that thousands of individuals become victims of scams similar to these. In fact, most of the victims never even meet the seller eyeball to eyeball. This is because many of the scams are successfully negotiated over the telephone!

BUYING AN EXISTING VENDING COMPANY

This is a classic "come on" for many business opportunity operations. The scam operation will place a classified advertisement stating that there is a route available in your territory. However when you call, you may discover that they are only planning on creating a route as soon as you have made the decision to send them the money to organize and establish the route in question! They will occasionally even begin placing certain types of equipment such as gumball machines on a new route. They use the same few machines to lure numerous unsuspecting investors, with the promise that there are many more accounts available. You will be advised that you must immediately secure the "exclusive territory." This needs to be done in order that they may begin the process of giving you the accounts that are established and also to collect your money promptly. They will convince you that they will secure the additional vending machines for the many other accounts that are waiting patiently just for you! If only life were that true and simple!

It is absolutely unbelievable to learn all the various sales pitches that these unscrupulous organizations use. It is even more astounding to hear about the number of individuals who allow themselves to be led into a totally losing proposition!

Of course, there are legitimate vendors who occasionally attempt to sell their routes through the classified ads. Some of these individuals or corporations are frequently selling out completely and retiring from vending. Others may be attempting to sell a portion of their route for a variety of reasons. However this is not a frequest occurence.

You should still exercise just as much caution in these situations. In actuality, there are individuals who attempt to buy and sell routes with little regard for the success of the seller from whom they are buying or the investor to whom they are selling. Some of these sales people, who pose as established vending operators, even use written guarantees to assure you that your new locations will be secure for a specified period of time. If this is not sufficient assurance, some will offer lifetime guarantees! What will they think of next? That is like buying a used car from a shady used car salesman who is offering you a lifetime warranty on the used car! Would you really believe that? If you do, then you truly deserve the blight that awaits you. Better yet, maybe I should sell you some "tropical beachfront" property in Kansas!

BUYING VENDING MACHINES SPORADICALLY

Potential vending machine investors occasionally see equipment at auctions, garage sales, in newspaper advertising and magazines. In spite of your limited knowledge of vending, you may find it attractive to buy such units because they are cheap.

Later, when you discover that parts are no longer available or there is no one that will repair the machines or worse, if they do, it cost significantly more than the entire cost of the machine, you will truly fall apart...along with the extinct vending machine you bought!

You will quickly find that keeping the bargain machine in operating condition can be costly, time consuming and utterly frustrating. Before long, the units are sacrificed or in many cases abandoned or junked. This does not mean that older machines are not a good investment. The trick is, knowing which machines you should buy and from which ones you should stay clear. As the years pass, these decisions will also have to be adjusted accordingly. Sound consultation is priceless in such situations.

LOCATING COMPANIES

Many business opportunity outfits will use locating companies to fulfill some of the outrageous promises that they have made, including the assurance that you would collect substantial sums of cash from your cash pans. However, later on, the very locating company who was once referred by the seller of the vending machines may quickly present disclaimers regarding the business opportunity outfit that sent you to them! The sales company who sold you the machines will also offer disclaimers regarding the locating companies. Everyone involved will be trying to cover their own rear ends!

Typically very few of these alliances will take total responsibility for what is about to happen to you, the new investor. Locating companies usually request their money up front. They will promise you extraordinary and convincing guarantees in order receive the payment immediately. For example; they will assure you that you are going to get prime locations, or they will promise to find you additional locations, or if necessary, another locating company! This is frequently comforting to the investor because it appears as though nothing could possibly go wrong! If you believe them, then remind me to tell you about some more bargain tropical ocean front property in the State of Iowa!

Frankly speaking, there are legitimate locating companies that are available to serve you. Many of these companies are best known via references from other vending companies. I sometimes refer locators to my customers but I continue to monitor the comments from my vendors to insure that the locators remain honest.

Most locators specialize in specific vending equipment that they handle. Be sure to determine the specialty of the locator before you tell her what type of vending equipment you desire locating!

"FALSE" PRODUCT SECURITY

Most scam artists will promote Hershey, M&M's. Coca-Cola, Nestle and a wide variety of other nationally recognized products as a lure to get the potential investor to make the first phone contact. Later, these reputable household product names are used to give authenticity to the entire sales pitch. In many cases the candy manufacturers are not even aware of how their names are being used or the exact nature of the sales pitch used by these scams. Consequently, high profile manufacturers are frequently unwilling to endorse such business opportunity sales organizations.

NECESSARY PRECAUTIONS

Whatever you do, never let anyone rush you to close a deal. Never assume that the seller will be there to offer you backup and support, based upon their say-so. Never allow the big product manufacturer names to convince you or move you closer to a comfort zone to close a deal.

Beware of organizations that demand your cashier's check to be sent immediately by Federal Express. You should question why they might frequently promise to ship your equipment in 60 to 90 days. There is a possibility that you may never receive any equipment whatsoever!

Once you are on your own, it is quite likely that the accounts your locator provided may become your worst nightmare. Before long, you may not receive any returned calls from the original seller or the locator because your expectations may not be considered "reasonable." Moreover, the business opportunity outfit that sold you the "goods" will more than likely remind you that they are only answerable for the sale of the equipment but not the locating! It is also not prudent to believe that you will have an exclusive territory as promised!

Check the credibility of the establishment you are dealing with. I will offer some pointers on how to do this later as you read on.

Chapter 3

TYPES OF VENDING MACHINES

There are many types of vending machines in the marketplace. These range from small table top mechanical peanut vending machine units that only accept one denomination of coin such as a quarter, to the most sophisticated electronic equipment. These advanced vending machines may be all inclusive, combination coffee, snack, food and soda machines in one cabinet that can practically do backward flips and shake your hand! The following is a brief description of the various types of vending machines:

BULK VENDING

This category includes the small vending machine units that may be placed individually or on racks with dozens of units placed together, on a custom welded framework. There are capsules, toys, snacks, games, candy, cards and a host of similar units that dispense small items that are included in this category. You will find giant gumball machines that light up and have recorded messages and simple machines that are extremely basic.

Most of the machines in this category are exclusively mechanical. The advantage to buying these machines is the cheap prices and the high profit potential. They are small and easy to locate, store, and transport. The down side is the risk involved due to vandalism and fraudulent use of coin substitutes. Inventory control is not as much a science as the more sophisticated vending machines. Theft of the entire bulk machine is far more possible and likely to occur than a machine that weighs one ton! Therefore you would need to place the machines in secure locations and not at the back door of an establishment or on a dock area!

CANNED, BOTTLED AND CUP BEVERAGE VENDING MACHINES

These are available in small tabletop units in both mechanical and electronic models. They are capable of dispensing a wide variety of popular colas and juices. Some vendors specialize in healthy drinks and even alcoholic beverages. Canned beverage vending machines are the most popular vending machines in this category.

On an average, these canned beverage-vending units offer three to ten selections. The cup soda machines are more complicated and offer multiple size cups. Sanitation is more of a concern with cup soda than the other style canned beverage dispensers.

Some units dispense cups automatically while others provide an area for the patron to place a cup prior to making a selection. Machines may dispense 6 oz, 8 oz, 10 oz, 12 oz, 16 oz, 20 oz, 36 oz or other size servings in cans, cups, plastic or glass containers. There are an ever-increasing variety of choices for consumers. If you try to offer all the options, you may face some serious challenges! Try to focus on one or two methods and stick with those. Some vendors like to vend canned beverages exclusively. Others like 20 oz bottles exclusively. Some offer a combination of both.

SNACK, PASTRY AND CANDY VENDING

More and more small business locations are seeking out small vending companies that are eager to place snacks, pastry and candy vending machines at their accounts. These vending machines are available in tabletop electronic and mechanical styles. Mechanical machines are always less expensive than electronic units. However no machine is completely free of problems as many eager vending sales scam artists may have you believe. However, there is a time and place for each style of vending equipment.

These machines can have as little as five or six or as many as eighty selections. Each selection may hold as little as five or six items or as many as eighteen to forty items. When a new customer looks through our *World's First Vending Machine Price Catalog*, it is always amusing to hear the dismaying comments they make when they first discover the wide varieties of vending machine styles and options that are listed in the catalog! What they thought was about to be a simple decision, becomes a new study and adventure that they were not expecting. While some decide to make an exit at this point, others roll up their sleeves in the exciting anticipation to move forward!

COLD FOOD

These large vending machines are capable of vending sandwiches, fruit, dairy products, juice, canned entrees, complete meals, desserts and a host of similar products that usually have a limited shelf life. These machines are extremely expensive and a vendor has to be very selective when placing these units in order to avoid heavy losses. A novice vendor may not want to jump in and place cold food vending machines unless they were fortunate enough to secure a very large account. Food machines need more detailed attention and perishable products have to be handled differently to all the other products such as candy, gumballs, chips, canned and bottled beverages and so on.

FROZEN FOOD AND DESSERT

Although these vending machines have been available for many years, it is only very recently that a strong renewed interest has been resurfacing. Today, these units are no longer available with only three or four selections. There are full sized, coin operated, frozen glass front merchandisers, similar to the popular snack and candy glass front units. These frozen units offer wide varieties of frozen foods and desserts. Of course, high price tags go along with such machines, the products that they dispense not to mention the handling and transportation. I would caution you to think carefully about these machines as much as you would a regular cold food machine. The only advantage of the frozen machine over the refrigerated is that you do not have to worry as much about the product quickly expiring!

TOBACCO AND RELATED PRODUCTS

It is quite evident that the future of cigarette vending may very rapidly be approaching the end of an era, as we have known it over the past fifty years. There is now much controvery about this type of vending. However, these units are still being manufactured and are now available in the latest glass front styles, similar to the snack, candy and frozen units.

Tobacco Marts are capable of merchandising not only cigarettes, like their older mechanical counterparts used to do, but the newest units merchandise cigars, chewing tobacco, cigarette lighters, exotic pipes and pipe tobacco. They are still manufactured in both mechanical and electronic styles.

There are new introductions of small table top or wall mounted versions created exclusively for dispensing cigars and/or cigarettes and may also be purchased with optional humidors to keep the products ultra fresh!

As long as there are smokers, night clubs, bars, casinos and other reasons to reach for a convenient pack of smokes…there will be a vending machine somewhere in a corner of such establishments. The owner of such equipment will most likely to be struggling to meet the latest stringent legal guidelines to maintain the machine in operation.

HOT BEVERAGES

Once upon a time, there was only one item you could buy from a hot beverage vending machine . . . coffee. Times have changed and there is a new revolutionary trend in how hot beverages are dispensed from a vending machine. There are tabletop units ranging from the least complicated, single pot style, to the highly sophisticated tabletop and also full size hot beverage dispensing machines. These large units are capable of vending, cappuccino, espresso and hot chocolate. They also dispense tea, decaffeinated coffee, hot cider, soup, exotic flavors and, oh yes, regular coffee! These units offer multiple size cups and many are capable of dispensing your choice of a specially formulated paper cup or allowing you to place your own favorite cup from home. Some machines offer bean grinders that grind the beans for exactly one cup of coffee at a time! Now that is service! However, keep in mind that the more sophisticated the vending machine, the more you may have to learn about maintaining the intricate details and operations of said equipment.

MISCELLANEOUS VENDING EQUIPMENT

There are dollar changers and vending machines capable of changing $1 $2 $5 $10 and $20 bills. These range from tabletop units that hold less than one hundred dollars in change, to monster units that hold thousands of dollars in change. Coin operated units in the market place include pay phones, stamp machines, parking lot meters, laundry mats, portable and full size standard car washes, coin operated microwave ovens, perfume machine dispensers, tooth paste dispensers, condom vending machines, feminine napkin dispensers, kiddie rides, atm's, phone card dispensers, cranes, games, impulse and many other.

TYPES OF COIN MECHANISMS

Every vending machine must accept and verify the coin, currency or other monetary method used, in order to dispense a product. The average newcomer to the vending industry is usually intrigued and in some cases challenged by the wide variety of mechanisms that are available on vending machines.

Mechanical coin mechanisms are very basic and accept the exact change only. Some machines are designed to accept only one denomination. For example, a gumball machine usually will accept only a "quarter". Other mechanical machines will accept Quarters, Nickels and Dimes. However, you must place the exact amount of each denomination in the correct slot as identified in the directions on the coin mechanism or on the front panel of the machine.

Electro mechanical machines combine the features of both mechanical operations such as pulling a handle outward and pushing it back in to receive a product. Of course this will only be possible after inserting a combination of coins into an electronic coin acceptor and receiving change below.

Electronic machines normally accept any combination of coins in any order. These machines will also return the correct change. Dollar bill acceptors are popular in the modern world of vending, allowing patrons to bypass an independent and separate dollar changer unit to break a large note. This strategy will therefore easily eliminate one extra step in the vending process. The currency is inserted directly into the vending machine and a purchase is made. The small change is promptly returned after the purchase.

Just when we thought we had all the up to date vending machine technology we could possibly handle, more advanced technology began lifting us to new heights. *Debit cards, charge cards* and other sophisticated methods of purchasing from vending machines are rapidly becoming the new standard in the world of vending. Vending machines can verify sales and do self-diagnostics and repairs via a telephone modem. A vending machine may be fifty or one hundred miles away from the vending company's headquarters, yet technicians are now capable of repairing the machine by remote control! In fact the vending machine may be on the other side of our planet and the same service could be administered. There is simply no end to the excitement and exuberance the industry is now experiencing as we move beyond 2000.

NOTES

Chapter 4
TYPES OF VENDING SERVICES

The average vending machine patron and the general public may not fully comprehend the methods or varieties of vending plans and programs. At best, they can relate to the insertion of their money into the machine and making a selection. This chapter will provide an overview of the most basic types of vending services: Full Service - Co-Operative Service (Co-Op Service) - Location Owned (Owner Operator) – Office Coffee Service (OCS) – Amusement Service and some others. Following is a brief outline of each main category.

FULL SERVICE VENDING

This method is by far the most popular method of vending services. The vending company, or the vending machine operator, owns the vending machines and contracts with the location to place the vending machines and related equipment on their location, at either no charge, or in exchange for a small commission payable to the location. The commissions are usually negotiable. The vendor assumes responsibility for all of the following: product purchases, refunds, repairs, spoilage, service calls, insurance, transportation, emptying the money pans, maintaining all vending machine keys, accountability details, and of course scheduling and staffing as necessary.

All items are sold at regular retail prices. The vendor deducts the true wholesale cost of goods and other related expenses and keeps the remaining profits. The location enjoys a truly "no obligation service" and has no investment responsibilities in the project. There is commonly a contract confirming the basic details of the agreement once both parties agree on the terms of the deal.

Some large locations require a cafeteria-style operation. Many large vending operations offer a complete vending and food service program. Due to the significant amount of corporate down sizing across the nation, these large locations that once supported very lucrative cafeterias, have found that it is no longer attractive to large vending operations to take over the accounts without a substantial location subsidy. Keep in mind that when larger locations demand cafeteria-style service, the vending machine sales and profits are not enough to cover the usual losses of a small cafeteria operation, and the location must provide a subsidy or give in to having a complete replacement of the cafeteria with *full service vending*!

CO-OP SERVICE VENDING

Some location managers prefer to get involved with the vending service by attempting to earn more money than what they presume a meager commission from Full Service may offer. Therefore, they sometimes agree to rent the vending machines from the vendor, and purchase all the necessary supplies from the vendor at prices somewhat higher than true wholesale. In some cases, the vending machines and related equipment such as microwaves, condiment stands, tables, chairs and so on, are placed at no charge. The vendor will deliver the products to the location and the management and staff at the location buy the products by the case. The location management will then make arrangements to handle the filling, cleaning and general service of the vending machines. They also store the products, count and deposit the money, decide exactly what they want to order and also keep the keys to the vending machines. They are trained to do minor repairs, but the vendor will respond if major repairs are necessary. The vendor may also choose to absorb the charges for major repairs except in the case of vandalism. Location managers who may not have a sufficient volume of sales to warrant a full service-vending program frequently select this program. The disadvantage of this pro gram for the location is that it does not earn as much money as the location manager may anticipate.

LOCATION OWNED VENDING

When the management of a location decides that they would like to have complete control over their vending service, including equipment and product selection, the management has the option of purchasing the vending equipment. This is where many locations make major errors. They are not properly educated with regard to the myriad of products and supplies. They are also lacking in the knowledge of the wide variety of equipment, the resulting responsibility and the accountability systems that are necessary to make it a successful venture.

If the location should choose this option, management is frequently willing to purchase the products from a vendor or directly from a wholesale outlet. Should the equipment malfunction, the location is responsible for finding a vending repair technician. They are not likely to find one that will respond with the urgency they could expect from a *full service vending* operation. Also the location is now subject to the varying charges that will be assessed.

If a machine has to be removed for repairs, the location will not have a temporary replacement offered promptly at no charge. There are locations that have chosen this option, only to recognize later on that they truly miss their *full service vending* option. They may decide to negotiate to have a vending operator return and service their equipment on a Full Service basis! Prices of the products being sold may have to be renegotiated at that time. However, the *owner operators'* choice can be a lucrative option if the location management has received sufficient consultation on the subject and are capable of handling the routine described above. There are thousands of organizations that enjoy this option. They make quite a tidy profit using company owned vending machines. The profits usually fund the annual dinners, ball games, summer BBQ events and other similar festivities.

Chapter 5

THE 12 COMMANDMENTS OF VENDING

By now you must have concluded that good vending service does not just happen by accident! It is considered by everyone inside and outside of our industry to be a professional management function. Contrary to some thinking, you do not merely buy a few vending machines, throw them on a location and sit back expecting the coins to start rolling in by the bucket loads!

Like most industries, vending has basic requirements, specifications, guidelines and rules that are necessary for you to heed if the business is to be successful. I like to refer to these fundamentals as the 12 Commandments of Vending.

1- Capital Investment
2- Proper Training
3- Orderly Scheduling
4- Stocking Parts and Products
5- Service and Repair
6- Preventive Maintenance
7- Merchandising for Success
8- Detailed Tracking
9- Cleanliness (Is next to Godliness)
10- Sensitivity to Consumer Desires
11- 24 Hour Service
12- Dress for Success

1 - CAPITAL INVESTMENT

It is not only the amount of the investment for the vending machine and related equipment that is important, but also the quality of such investment. It is important to invest in the most reliable modern machines, vans trucks, coin counting equipment, repair facilities, accounting and other equipment, hand trucks and packaging machinery. In order to accomplish all this, it requires experience; know how, and above all, careful management of the vending company's assets.

Periodically the operator may find it necessary to use refurbished vending equipment and vehicles. This is quite acceptable where it has been determined that such equipment and vehicles are adequate for the circumstances.

Regardless of how much money you may have, it will never be enough. You will always find a need to have more capital to expand your business as you begin to grow and prosper. Unless you grow very slowly and wait for your equipment to completely pay off and then buy more equipment, you will surely have to become creative in this aspect of business. Evaluating the new accounts and projecting the income necessary to make the proper capital investment is crucial.

Most scam operations will promise you the moon and the stars. For example, they express that they will sell you a vending machine for $2000 and that you will make $5,000 to $10,000 in a very short period of time. You need to be practical and determine what you expect to be the very minimum return on your investment. Once you have made such a determination you may evaluate the prospective location and make the right move.

There are a variety of methods that can be used to determine how much capital investment should be necessary when you are considering a vending machine business. The criteria may be totally different than those needed when buying a money counting machine, a truck, office furniture, a computer or other similar items. I will gladly expand on issues like these with vendors who desire more detailed analysis with respect to specific applications and circumstances. I will also discuss related topics in more detail throughout this book and in some of my seminars and personalized consultation sessions.

At Hanna, financing is quickly arranged for established customers and new vendors. Credit repair services are also offered in an attempt to clear up any blemishes that may appear on a credit history. By having an excellent credit rating you will be ready to expand your vending operation successfully.

2 - PROPER TRAINING

There is no such thing as "enough training". A professional vending service operator is always willing to learn more about the control settings of various machines, how much products to load, the coin mechanism levels necessary to function properly, setting prices and the correct product sizes to fit special augers or dispensing mechanisms and so on.

Whether you are a one-person operation or a major corporation, you must continue to sharpen your skills and the skills of those who are working in your environment. It is the simple routines in this business, which are often taken for granted. When these routines are neglected they always end up costing us dearly. As you already know, anything that is worth doing...is worth doing right.

If you have manuals that explain the proper working of a particular piece of equipment you should read it carefully and become familiar with the details to the best of your ability. Sometimes the distributor, vendor or manufacturer from whom you buy vending equipment may be willing to offer some hands on training. While this is not always necessary, be willing to take advantage of such offers.

3 - ORDERLY SCHEDULING

It is imperative that the service schedule is effective and orderly. This will insure that each installation is ready for the coffee or lunch break. Coordinating the kitchen and warehouse operation with the destinations of the service trucks and having the right inventory of cups, candy bars, cigarettes, soda, juice and sandwiches on hand are all part of the service company's daily routine.

A professional vending company runs like an airline or a first-class hotel, getting everything to the right place or person at the right time. Some small vending operators tend to service their accounts whenever they feel like it. The customer can sense the end result of such sloppy service. They will not be able to rely on a schedule that would demonstrate a degree of professionalism on the part of the vending operator.

If you decide that a particular account needs to be serviced only once per week, decide on a day (or days) of the week and preferably mornings or afternoons then stick to that schedule. As your business grows your time will become more precious to you and you should learn to plan your days more effectively while your customers are demanding more from you also. This careful scheduling and planning will also help you to evaluate the quality of the account and the income that is derived from it, because the collections are being made on a consistent basis.

4 - STOCKING PARTS AND PRODUCTS

Pleasing your customers will only be possible if you stock and provide their favorite products at all times. Therefore a careful study should be made to determine not only the best-selling products in the marketplace but the special requests that your customers are demanding. The warehouse or garage area from where you will operate should be organized with an inventory of items, always readily available for loading onto the service vehicle.

This principle, when fully understood, helps to guarantee the availability of important "back up" spare parts for both vending machines and service vehicles to insure minimum down time. We all know that time is money. A 50cents part has been known to cause a vending machine to malfunction, which could lead to tens or hundreds of dollars of losses in sales, not to mention customer frustration and possible loss of the entire account!

Certain vending machine parts may be the same for some vending machines wherever you are in the USA or other parts of the world. The same switch or motor for a specific year and model beverage vending machine will normally work on all identical American-made beverage vending machines successfully.

However, one should not confuse or compare the strategy of using the same vending machine parts or setting successfully all over the world with a similar assumption that most vendible products may fit in all beverage vending machines. In fact, product sizes for items sold in vending machines may vary substantially and create certain problems when inserted in vending machines. For example, a specific can of soda, in one country may have a totally different set of dimensions to a similar product in another country.

In addition to the above points, other factors are to be considered. For example, Pepsi Cola may sell much better in one geographic area while Coca-Cola might out sell Pepsi in another area. Along with stocking the best selling products, you have to be absolutely sure that you are also stocking the right vending machine parts. This will insure that your machines are exposed to a minimum amount of down time while stocking edible products that will turn over frequently in the area that you are operating your business. You will be able to determine in a short period of time the proper amount of equipment parts and ideal product mix that will assure maximum customer satisfaction at all times.

5- SERVICE & REPAIR

A smart vending machine operator or route driver is always alert for signs of potential problems regarding his vending and related equipment at his/her account. The manner in which products are placed in a vending machine, determines whether the product will dispense successfully or not. However there are numerous other factors that may determine how well the equipment will function.

In some circumstances the problem may be as simple as someone placing money in a coin mechanism to vend a product, however, due to a distraction, the customer may not have consummated the deal. Hence, forgetting to press the required button on the machine and walking away causes the machine to be rendered out of order unless someone knew what happened. Later, after the customer has left the location, the next customer who walks up to the machine, may become frustrated to discover that his coins are running through to the "return change cup". The machine has not forgotten that someone needed to push the button and complete the sale that was not handled properly earlier! I have seen and heard about hundreds of service calls whereby the technician or route driver drove forty to fifty miles to a location in response to a service call request. When they arrived at the location to repair the machine, they discover that the only problem with the machine was that no one had pushed the button to release a product!

When an owner operator is running her own business and does all the work, she does not have to worry about most of the issues that a major corporate Operation's Manager is faced with on a daily basis. When a driver is hired to run a route and fill vending machines, there is a good chance that the vending company may find some genuinely conscientious, hard working and dedicated employees. However, when a route driver decides that she simply wants to get in and out and rush the job, this creates serious problems for the vending machine owners. Why? Because if a driver is not as dedicated as she should be, the machine may not be filled to the right levels, doors may not be shut and locked securely, "test vends" may not have been conducted, coin mechanisms not cleaned or tested and visual inspections not completed! More important, she may not be checking with the receptionist or main contact for refunds or complaints and such important matters may be totally ignored!

Customers or the location contact need clear instructions that they should follow if the vending machine malfunctions. They should also be aware of the schedule for servicing of the equipment that you have placed on their location. If you receive a call for repair of a vending machine you should be prepared to respond within the time frame that you promised. For example: You may inform your customer that you will guarantee a response within 24 hours or sooner and in most cases you will handle the complaint within three to six hours. If you have a rigid schedule for filling your vending machines you will not have to anticipate any complaints regarding empty machines. The only potential complaints will be the occasional malfunction, which entails the removal of a damaged coin from the coin mechanism or a product that has jammed the machine and so on!

6- PREVENTIVE MAINTENANCE

Everything made by mankind will eventually break down. Just like cars, planes, trucks, forklifts, lawn mowers, boats and other similar machinery, vending machines need regular maintenance schedules to hold interruption of service to a minimum. Some machines need a minimal amount of service while others require more rigid maintenance. Obviously, simple manual vending machines do not demand the attention that advanced electronic equipment does. This should not lead you to believe that one type of machine may be better than the other.

The one thing on which we all could easily agree is that preventive maintenance is less expensive than major breakdowns. Routine inspection of switches, solenoids, coin mechanisms, dollar validators, large and small moving parts, electrical cords, machine temperature and dispensing mechanisms are easy to do. Most machines are easily rendered "out of order" due to simple matters such as dirty coin mechanisms.

7- MERCHANDISING FOR SUCCESS

Who said that successful merchandising through vending machines is totally automatic? This is simply not true. It is imperative that foods, beverages, snacks and other vendible products are displayed attractively and in the correct column or shelf position. Products have to be rotated on a rigorous schedule and special attention should be directed toward the placement of appealing packages in the machines and in some form of color coordination. This is a major challenge for owners and managers of professional vending companies all over the world in order to enhance customer satisfaction during the final moments of the prospect deciding what or if they should buy from the machine.

Simple strategies such as taking a survey and determining exactly what the customers want at their location vending machines can be very important. There are always going to be universal best-selling items in certain countries or geographic areas. For example, in Kansas City and most cities in the USA it would be foolish not to offer certain powerful sellers such as Snickers or M&M's. However, a few dedicated slots should always be reserved for special requests from the specific location and especially in certain geographic areas. A good example would be placing a snack vending machine in a Hispanic area in Miami, Florida compared to placing a snack machine in a predominantly suburban Kansas City location. The Florida location may request certain items such as Banana Chips and other similar popular cultural choices while the Kansas City location may opt for a local brand **BBQ** chips and so on.

The machines should always be full, clean and working. When you walk up to a vending machine of your choice, and you already have a desire to purchase a beverage or a snack item, it is likely that you will do so in a satisfied manner. On the other hand, having to settle for an inferior selection from a half empty, dirty machine would not be good for future business and the vending machine owner will suffer the financial consequences. Proper pricing decals and flavor strips must always be in their respective slots. Specials may be placed on the machines to promote a certain item or draw attention to "low fat" items, salt free,100% juice or other similar trendy or expected choices.

The position of the products being placed within the machine can also determine the success of the sales. Some items are better at eye level and others are better located where the distance of the drop to the dispensing tray is the least and most desired to deliver a product that remains in tact! For example, who would want to buy a cherry pie that fell from the top draw of the snack machine and splattered all over the delivery tray below?

Similar principles apply to any other type of vending machines. So far, I have been mentioning mostly beverage and snack machines. However, the same quality merchandising techniques apply when servicing other vending machines such as coffee, phone cards, medicine, ice cream, condom, tampons, bubble gum, stamps, pencils and so on.

You must first attract the customer to your vending machine, have the price stated clearly, describe the product or have it clearly visible and have the correct decals. Maintaining attractive and clean vending machines will hold the customer's attention and ultimately earn their business. You are not always available at the machine to urge the customer to buy, therefore you have to prepare and properly arm your vending machine to be the ultimate "super sales robot" that it is.

8- DETAILED TRACKING

Monitoring details of a vending operation is not a matter to be taken lightly. Accountability and controls are of vital importance and makes the difference between success and failure in any organization, especially in vending. These details include everything from organizing the warehouse (garage, house, or apartment) to loading the truck (van, or car) to stocking the machines and collecting the cash. The chain of controls may be simple or sophisticated but should be monitored literally by the minute depending on the size of the operation.

Whenever commissions are being offered to a location, good vending service also means an accounting to the client regularly and accurately about sales, costs and profit margins. These detailed functions separate the professional vendor from the novice.

Manual record keeping can be simple to maintain and is sufficient if the business is fairly small. However, there are very inexpensive computer vending software packages for your basic personal computer system that may save you many unnecessary difficulties with initial details and may very well be worth the small investment to allow such programs to guide your efforts.

It is imperative that you track the items that are selling better than others and rotate in new selections to replace the slow selling items. The difference between a lazy route driver and a driver who has a vested interest in sales can be tied directly to the frequency with which he tries new items to replace slow sellers in the vending machine.

Tracking your service calls can save you from losing your account. When a machine malfunctions frequently, it is effortless to remedy the problem and forget about it until the next time it malfunctions and frustrates the customer. If the details of these service calls are not monitored and studied, you will never be able to accurately determine, by process of elimination, exactly what action to take next. More important, when the customer demands an explanation about the frequency in the interruption of service it will be impossible to professionally describe the precise actions taken in the past coupled with the actions that are being taken immediately to correct such problems.

When you perform technical assistance or repairs, it is of great importance to have such matters documented in detail. Such detailed tracking should include dates and corrective actions already taken. This will help you or your technician to make an intelligent assessment of the real problems being experienced now and in the future. It is only with such tracking that one can make a final decision to repair or replace a machine with confidence.

9- CLEANLINESS (IS NEXT TO GODLINESS)

Enough cannot be said about scrupulous sanitation of vending machines. Because many vended products are perishable, very strict adherence to freshness, machine cleanliness and sanitation regulations is another compelling ingredient of superior vending service. Therefore you should take time to become properly trained in this area to assure continued effective supervision as you grow and hopefully prosper.

A simple step, such as cleaning the glass front of a snack merchandiser, will increase sales and give much confidence to the consumer standing in front of the machine while pondering what or if they should buy! A dirty machine is an indication of a dirty operator and more alarming, the possibility of non-hygienic or unsanitary products inside the machine. As you already know, first impressions are lasting, and when your customers walk up to the vending machine, you should always feel confident that they will be impressed, motivated and comfortable to make a rapid purchase.

Certain machines necessitate more attention than others, if safety concerns are to be minimized. For example, coffee vending machines would need more frequent cleaning and sanitation attention than a canned beverage vending machine. Hot and cold food machines will need more attention than a snack and candy machine. However they all need to be cleaned and sanitized at intervals that are acceptable for the style and type of vending machine.

While most customers cannot see inside the vending machines most of the time, an operator should never be embarrassed to keep his vending machine door open while servicing the machine even if there are dozens of customers standing around. One bad impression can cause a significant drop in sales and lowered confidence in the vending machine operator.

You guessed it. Bad news travels fast! It is much more difficult to regain the confidence from location management once it is lost and in most cases they find it easier to switch vending companies than complain repeatedly. They do this to demonstrate their concern for their employees.

10- SENSITIVITY TO CONSUMER DESIRES

We all know that nothing remains constant and change is inevitable with regard to everything within this universe. Therefore, never conclude that consumer desires are all alike or that they will all remain the same! Like the department stores and supermarkets, prosperous vending organizations must constantly monitor customer preferences and requests.

Your responses to simple consumer concerns about the strength and temperature of the coffee, types of salads, selections of candy bars, chips, pastry, dairy product choices, healthy items and other sensitive preferences may determine whether you wind up losing an account. However your positive action will make them so happy that they gladly refer you to more business than you can handle.

Therefore, if a favorite candy bar is out of stock or the latest health beverage product is on back order, you must communicate with your customers to assure that their special requests are being taken seriously and that you are quick and eager to respond. Communication is the key. Keeping in touch with your contact person should be one of the most important routines you can possibly perform.

The main contact is the thermometer and main indicator of your degree of stability with the account. Most account contacts can be very forgiving and understanding as long as the level and frequency of communication demonstrates the genuine concern and diligence of the vending operator.

Once in a while a location contact may request an item that you already know is not a good seller or even worthy of placement. However, it is the manner in which these requests are handled that will determine the quality of the relationship of location and vendor. I have found that when I express my sincere feelings that the product requested will not be a good seller but that I am willing to take a loss to give it the benefit of the doubt, the customer feels extra special. In fact, I find it much easier to remove the product successfully once I can demonstrate the results of the tracking of the sales of that particular product.

I have actually lost accounts and never really knew the reason until some time afterward. For example, a manager at one of my accounts approached one of my route drivers and asked for a certain product. My route driver simply stated that it was a lousy seller and that we merely would not place such a product in the machine. Suddenly, in the manager's mind, it was no longer the product that was perceived to be lousy but he assumes that the driver's opinion of him was that "he/she" the manager was lousy. The driver may not have been sensitive enough to handle the situation properly and I lost a $50,000 account due to such insensitivity from a driver who probably wanted to get home early that day. His intentions may have been to reach a friend's party on time, never thinking that he did or said anything wrong. It is not what we say but how we say it that makes all the difference in the world!

11- 24 HOUR-SERVICE

You guessed it . . . vending machines do not sleep or take vacations. You are running a 24-hour 365 days per year operation! A vending service company must be ready, in most cases, to keep the vending machines operational every minute of every day. Consumers expect and demand it, and sales will certainly suffer without it.

If you are not able to take telephone calls personally, consider an answering machine with a professional message, answering service, hand-held phone or a pager. Let the customer know exactly how serious and dedicated you are to SERVICE. Anyone can sell cola or candy from a vending machine, but it takes special personalized attention to detail if you are to be successful.

12- DRESS FOR SUCCESS

Walking into your customer's location in jeans and a sweatshirt, says a lot about who you are and what you are not! You never see the US Mail delivery person or any of the professional delivery route personnel from other reputable organizations dressed sloppily, do you? Of course not! The image they want to impress upon their customers and potential customers is integrity, professionalism, cleanliness, organization, uniformity and dependability. You should attempt doing the same thing whenever possible. Always dress for success!

It is not expensive to dress in a uniformed manner and to allow the customer to associate you with a certain degree of respect for your professionalism. They want to be proud to have you walk into their place of business and also to have a feeling of security with some degree of stability. Whether you decide to wear regular black slacks and clean a white shirt or khaki pants and green shirt, be consistent and if possible, formalize the outfits with your name and possibly your logo if you have one.

I have always chosen to dress with a shirt, tie and black or gray pants. When I first started out in vending and was running my own route, I was a one-man operation and had to be all things to all people at any given moment. I found that it was better to be over dressed than under dressed. There were times when I had to rent a truck, install a machine, then return to filling my machines and later meet a new prospect to convince him to allow me to become his vendor. Frequently, I would be driving along and decide to stop in on a location that seemed promising and I was never embarrassed to walk in and meet the receptionist . . . or the president of the company!

In the faddish times of the year 2000 and beyond, it appears that "casual" is the order of the day. Some organizations actually allow that and some do not. When in doubt, I always prefer to take what I believe to be the most appropriate approach. I would prefer not to offend or diminish the level of professional appearance that is necessary while I am conducting business with people at the top management level in their organizations.

When a vending organization is large enough to have route drivers, supervisors, technicians, operation and general managers or Vice Presidents and other management, it is a slightly different story. I am not suggesting that a route driver should wear a shirt and tie. It may be uncomfortable, unnecessary and sometimes dangerous to wear a tie just to keep the machines clean, full and working. However, it is more appropriate if you are running the company. When the owner operator is doing all the management and route work including purchasing and sales, he or she may want to look as professional and comfortable at the same time.

Grooming and hygiene is equally consequential. There is nothing more unpleasant than having a route service representative handling your food and having his scraggly hair in the products and his body odor and breath being noticeably repulsive. Would you want to buy from someone like that? No one wants to buy from a person with markedly dirty hands knowing that they have been handling the food you are about to consume. I have had some of the kindest and most decent employees, over the years, who had performed a fairly good job, thereby postponing my desire to correct their bad grooming and hygiene habits. Occasionally I was forced to let such employees go after repeated requests for them to become more conscious of their poor hygiene habits. Eventually, I became less tolerant of such habits and implemented stricter policies regarding such matters.

Chapter 6

PRODUCT AND EQUIPMENT SUPPLY

There is no one central place to get everything you will need for every type of vending machine, vendible products, parts, training, consultation and service. There are literally hundreds of different types of vending and related vending machines, thousands of products and countless parts for all the varieties of vending equipment in the world.

When I first started my vending business in 1976, I was very frustrated in my search to find reliable, dependable, honest individuals or organizations to which I could turn for consultation, vending equipment and supplies. After getting ripped off initially on my first few vending machine purchases, buying products from several sources including grocery stores, drug stores and other vendors, I realized that there was no particular best deal at any one time. I learned that lesson the hard way.

I dreamed of how wonderful it would have been to have one central place to shop and be able to receive guidance along every step of the way. I had no idea at that time that The Hanna Company was actually destined to become one of the only such dedicated organizations of its kind in the world. For the next 25 years my company was transformed into everything I was looking for and could not find. I enjoyed those years very much because it allowed me the satisfaction of helping those, who would have been ripped off or discouraged, to continue in vending. It also afforded me the opportunity to become diversified offering a wide variety of vending related equipment, products and ser- vices.

After the successful sale of my multi million-dollar "full service vending division" in September 1999, I decided to maintain and expand my vending equipment sales company under a new name, The Hanna Group –Vending Equipment Sales&Service. I also maintained my credit repair services, tax referral services and other consultation services while I accepted a transitional management position at the company that acquired my local full service vending division.

The sale of my local division was truly the most scary and exciting moment in my life. I realized that I could help more vendors throughout the USA and the world by sharing my multitude of experiences with them. My customers would continue to be able to receive my vending consultation initially, followed by the purchase of the necessary vending and related equipment at the most competitive prices just as I had always offered during the previous twenty five years. I would also have the opportunity to help small and large vending companies, including the company that purchased my local full service vending division. I utilized my experience to help them build their full service vending company while building my own remaining divisions, which included vending equipment sales, consultation and related Hanna divisions that I had retained. Although I committed to only a six month transition management position I intend to assist in that project until they no longer have a need for my services and they become self sufficient within the market place.

Most important, I would continue to be an advocate against vending scams within the vending industry and prevent such scams in any way I could. I would also help those who may have already succumbed to such unscrupulous dealings.

Depending on the size of a vending company, there are numerous options available to operators. While Hanna offers a wide variety of vending machines, products, parts and consultation to operators all over the U.S. and the world, we recommend how and where the operators may want to guardedly examine additional choices available to them.

There are numerous business organizations everywhere that choose to own their vending machines without using a professional vending service company. Some of these organizations include car dealerships, banks, insurance companies, hospitals, retirement homes, service stations, convenience stores, grocery stores and many others. Most of these organizations may not always be aware of the considerable degree of detailed commitment such projects will necessitate.

There are some individuals in organizations such as those mentioned above, who conclude that vending is automatic and therefore the profits are automatic also! They soon discover that if there is no serious commitment to learning more about the intricate details of vending machine inventory control, purchasing, labor costs, equipment costs, storage of products, spoilage, petty theft and all the other related factors, they are only delaying the inevitable disaster that awaits them.

Those who do their homework will usually do well. However, in many cases, they become tired of the routine because there may not be enough profit due to limited sales volume to make it worth their time and effort. Ultimately it is a lack of sound basic management principles that would possibly subject the project to doom.

WHOLESALE CLUB OFFERS

I receive thousands of calls from individuals and corporations every year who request information on vending and how they may do it themselves. Once I determine their reasons for such inquiries we will usually make suggestions and recommendations for them to either seek a professional vending company or advise them on the other options available. Once they are properly educated from the very beginning, their chances of success increase substantially.

There is a handful of vending product wholesale outlets in most major cities across the country. Very little is available to vending machine operators in rural and smaller well-known cities. Wholesale clubs are also available in heavily populated areas. These types of operations do not cater to vending companies exclusively and therefore carry a limited variety of vending items of interest and popularity as needed by the professional vendor.

Some of these wholesale club outlets even attempt to sell vending machines to the general public. Most professional vendors know better than to buy vending machines from these organizations. For the most part, they realize that the equipment being offered may not only be inferior quality compared to the more stable line of equipment that may be used by professionals, but that there is no immediate and effective personalized "attention to detail" after the sale.

Individuals, who are lured, by the offer to start their own vending operations with specific vending machines, find such equipment irresistible only because they have never been properly educated about the numerous other vending options, which are available to established vendors.

Wholesale clubs are also not able to offer the consultation, account referrals, service, parts and the numerous other important benefits after the sale. In fact these stores usually end up referring the customer to someone else who may not always take responsibility for the equipment which was sold and which may possibly have been the wrong choice of equipment for the size of the location. This compounds the frustration of the small vendor or the location manager who thought that he or she was making the right decision to buy from a wholesale club outlet store.

Small vending operators are always on the look out for special discounted big brand vendible snack and beverage products. They seek these deals from reputable retail outlets, which some times sell these items for less than most wholesale outlets can buy the same products. Due to special incentive programs occasionally offered to these retailers by the product manufacturers, they are able to sell the promotional items as a lost leader and the product manufacturers may offer advertising allowances and shelf space allowances among other deals in exchange for rapid movement of products, they in turn benefit from the maximum exposure. It is in such matters that wholesale clubs may sometimes also be a good choice. Buying products at reduced prices for the vending machines is an on going challenge especially for the small operator who cannot afford to buy factory direct.

Larger vending organizations usually have a more sophisticated purchasing procedure than a small operator. Large vendors will not tolerate having their purchasing department personnel running all over town trying to buy products on specials. These larger organizations receive volume discounts from manufacturers along with rebates; incentive programs and other deals to encourage the vendor to maintain certain brands in vend positions.

THE WARS OF THE COLA GIANTS

Most of the major bottlers of the best-selling colas aggressively place their vending machines on locations and actually compete with vending operators in addition to competing with the various cola and uncola brands in their respective market place. The bottlers will sometimes agree to work closely with vendors or individual retail locations who are willing to place loaner units (bottler identified) vending machines on locations and feature that bottler's brands exclusively. The bottlers are a source of supply to vendors who own and operate generic vending machines. Obviously, there are always competitive prices, as you have no doubt witnessed with the price wars of the cola giants over the years.

Prices of the dominant brands of colas fluctuate at wholesale depending on the status of the buyer. Some of the classifications for example separate schools, hospitals, vending companies, supermarkets, government establishments, fast food chains and other categories of businesses. There are more programs and levels of qualification than I could possibly cover in this book. The same is true of all major brands of snack, candy, food and other edible and non-edible vend products.

OTHER EQUIPMENT & PRODUCTS

The wide variety of vending equipment, products and services available, are also just as varied and complex as you read in the first part of this book. I am always amazed at the number of individuals who call me and ask questions such as: "I want to get into the vending business, which machine should I buy? Which is the best product to sell? How do I get locations? Where do I find the products? Who will fix my machines?" You can imagine how busy we have been, educating countless individuals who are normally very cxcited and ready to start immediately, until we share the hard facts and the realities of the vending industry. Only when we have determined that they are really committed and are truly ready, willing and able to handle an opportunity in vending will we encourage them to take the next step cautiously.

Please do not misunderstand our intentions about educating interested new vending opportunity prospects. I simply prefer NOT to tell anyone what he or she wants to hear but to tell him or her the way it really is! One of the reasons for writing this book was to offer a summary to those who were merely curious and also for those who already started out in vending but struggle to have a quick reference for the over all picture of the business. I receive numerous calls from government agencies in the USA and all over the world, libraries, business opportunity organizations, politicians, lawyers, district attorney offices and other similar organizations that are either trying to educate themselves or educate others in need.

WHEN YOU CANNOT OFFER IT ALL

I also assist major vending and other non-vending related corporations by educating them on many aspects of the vending industry with which they are not as yet familiar. In some instances, major vending companies may receive calls from a few of their enormous business accounts requesting a certain type of vending machine that the vending company does not routinely offer. These large vending companies would prefer not to get involved in every type of vending machine, products and services conceivable! Therefore requests for such varieties of vending equipment and services become a challenge for them.

I periodically receive calls from such established and reputable vending companies requesting that I send one of our price catalogs to their special customers in order that we may solve certain problems their customers are experiencing. We get involved with such customers of the vending company in order that their customers may easily purchase machines such as feminine napkin dispensers or medicine dispensers. We educate their location maintenance staff on how to do the service at the location in addition to the other routine services they normally do within the company restrooms and other parts of the building. This eliminates the large vending company from having to purchase and also service vending machines that are not a standard piece of equipment with which they desire or traditionally offer their customers.

These larger vendors are not concerned about Hanna selling to their accounts. Nor are they concerned that a shady vending operator or distributor may possibly rip off their customer! Above all else, the large vendor will be comfortable knowing that they will not be subjected to the possibility of referring their location to a potential competitor! Since most of these managers of larger vending companies know who is reputable in the vending industry and who is not, they will take the necessary action by turning to companies like Hanna and resolve the issues promptly. I have been most successful with many of these larger organizations and also various manufacturers and suppliers of vending and related equipment and have received hundreds of referrals annually based on their desire to satisfy their customers completely.

Vending machine manufacturers struggle with the concern of referring curiosity seekers to other manufacturers and distributors who may not be as reputable. They feel a responsibility to the serious prospects that are interested in what that manufacturer has to offer. However, in many cases they need to refer the prospect to a reputable source for the many other vending and related needs that they may be pursuing.

Chapter 7
MORE ON SCAMS

In Chapter 3 you read about detecting scams. I believe that it is important to elaborate more on this issue to show you just how simple or extremely sophisticated these ambitious "rip off" enterprises really can be. It may be necessary for me to repeat a few details during this and other chapters. One of my strongest reasons for writing this book was to shed some light on this ugly subject of vending scams. After I was scammed on my first purchase, I realized that I knew very little about my options. I had no idea what government agencies to turn to and frankly speaking, I was a bit embarrassed. Had I known that I could have called up the Better Business Bureau or the Office of The District Attorney of Kansas I would certainly have done that.

Several years later I accepted the fact that District Attorneys are real people just like you and I, they are available to protect us. I recognized that they could not help if they were not made aware of specific consumer related problems such as fraud, embezzlement, robberies and the numerous forms of crime that is prevalent in our communities. Since then, I successfully prosecuted several individuals who had been blatantly dishonest with me.

Some scams are little more than an ad in a newspaper offering a start up vending opportunity. A slick sales person quickly promises special territories to the new vendor in exchange for the purchase of a handful of vending machines. The new vendor prospect may be easily convinced to send their cash to the sales person and may eventually receive the machines or in many cases wind up receiving absolutely nothing whatsoever!

There are many, small time, "rip off artists" playing this game.

The pitch is believable to a certain degree, especially to a novice with no vending background. These con artists rarely approach individuals that are exposed to the vending industry. However, that is not always the case. The more sophisticated scams are truly a work of art and I believe that they deserve special attention to insure that you will not be easily plagiarized by such efforts. I will attempt to outline how a few of these scams may very well operate.

These scams are sometimes camouflaged as "Business Opportunities" or I may also refer to them as Bus-Op's for easy reference. They usually study a geographic area and target a particular group of prospects by level of income, business interests in previous business opportunity ventures, your subscriptions to business opportunity related magazines and newspapers, retirees or similar categories. They may then send out formal invitations to such prospects informing them that they have been "selected" to participate in a demonstration of a fool proof, recession proof and big money making opportunity. A deadline for your response and place of meeting is usually highlighted and a meeting place is established at a nearby reputable hotel in your neighborhood. You have to RSVP of course, because seats are always limited and you may miss out on the most important meeting of your life!

At the meeting, a very clever and organized team of sales experts, waste no time in putting on the best "dog and pony" show you could hope to witness. Some individuals, without delay, recognize the scam and promptly leave, or begin to ask too many questions and are encouraged to leave the meeting prematurely! They are ridiculed for asking such absurd questions because they are reminded that they are not qualified to comment on an industry that they obviously know nothing about. Besides, the sales staff would prefer not to discourage the remaining prospects by having them to listen to these negative comments. Before long, the meeting is divided into two groups. The individuals that are ready to learn more about how they can start in vending and the rest of the group who may wish to leave because they do not wish to listen to any more great Bus-Op presentations. Bottom line, some people are capable of seeing through scams very quickly! Once these people have left, the rest of the victims await their fate.

During this meeting you may have been convinced that the vending business is very easy. In fact, you will see repeated demonstrations of how easy it is to pull out the money pan full of coins! There will be much, "hands on" demonstrations and in some cases there may even be some "established customers" who are back for more and chomping at the bit to tell you how wonderful this opportunity will be for you too. By this time if you believe these "satisfied" customers, you will most likely be among the next victims that evening. You will be promised all training that is necessary to launch your new vending operation. You will even be taught how to maintain records, buy products, get parts and assistance any time you need it!

Bus-Op's may also offer to send you to their headquarters for a demonstration. They will pay for your airline ticket and even pick you up in a stretch limo! Some will also offer to pay your hotel bill. There is usually a catch. You may need to bring a cashier's check with you, "but you are not obligated to buy anything." If you believe that sales pitch, you are also in big trouble and maybe you would have an interest in purchasing some ocean front property in Lenexa, Kansas! ☺

The interested group is then taken to a "sit down," "roll up your sleeves" encounter with an opportunity for a "one on one" heavy duty "lets make a deal" closing discussion! The pressure is now applied for closing the sale, getting a deposit or the entire sales price, and then proceeding to the next town as quickly as possible. There are promises of the machines that will soon arrive. (Sometimes they do and sometimes they don't.) There are also promises of location specialists who are to arrive immediately after you receive your machines in order that they will get the machines into big money making and dynamite locations. These locators are usually never associated directly with the bus-op organization but simply recommended by them. (Sometimes they show up and sometimes they don't.) Whenever they do show up, the locations, which are negotiated on your behalf, are rarely ever what you may have been promised or that you may have been dreaming about!

By the time you decide to complain to the bus-op sales people, if you can still find them, they quickly remind you that they are not directly associated with the locating operation, as they had previously indicated. (While you were intoxicated with their pitch about how rich you were going to get!) At this time you probably begin to get a run around from both the locator and the Bus-Op sales office personnel. You will be reminded of the fine print in a contract that you signed. Out of desperation you start asking a lot of questions. By the time you have stumbled upon or have been referred to a legitimate organization, (Example. Local bottlers, local established vendors, district attorneys' office or Hanna) it is too late to recover your investment. Furthermore, you quickly realize that you have paid a significantly higher price than the vending equipment was actually worth!

Some of these Bus-Op organizations are usually new and have no long term-established references. They will direct your attention to the fact that they have never been reported to the Better Business Bureau. However, the reason they are comfortable using that line is due to the fact that they have not been operating long enough to have any reports filed. They already know that they probably will no longer be in business by the time the complaints are going to be filed.

Other organizations are very well established and follow a similar format. They may have a strong team of legal representatives that understand the importance of reminding you about the fact that you are an adult and that nothing was done to you that you did not agree to do, with signed contracts to boot! These guys are very slick and organized. Even their "references" are fantastic; in fact too good to be true . . . get it?

Frequently, even some of the manufacturers and distributors are aware of the scams. Manufacturers want to sell machines just like anyone else does. There is always a question of who the manufacturer really is! Some organizations claim to be manufacturers when in reality they are just assembling a portion of a machine or more realistically they are not doing anything but placing their own name on the machine after buying the equipment from an actual manufacturer or from a company that assembles equipment.

There are very few organizations that are considered THE manufacturer who makes every component of the vending machine they sell. However this is very rare. Instead, you will find that one company may make the body; another company makes the coin mechanisms while others make the coils or electrical harnesses and so on. Then the company who claims to be the manufacturer will actually be the company that is assembling the machines and placing their name on the units. They in turn sell the machines to independent distributors who sometimes place their own graphics or some other customized detail on the equipment to give the illusion that they are indeed the manufacturer. Therefore when a scam ends up in court, the scam artists may claim that they are not the actual manufacturers because they really are not at all involved in any aspect of the manufacturing or assembling of the units. They will also allude to the fact that they are not responsible for the locator who may also have ripped off the new vendor because they are a separate operation!

Over all the years that I have been in business, I have not been popular with certain individuals and organizations that would prefer that Hanna not share such details with the general public. In fact, we have been asked by some organizations to allow them to continue making a living by softening our position regarding scams. There are even some manufacturers who prefer to close an eye to the deliberate and devastating results of organized vending scams. Others threatened to discontinue selling to us and in a few cases, some of these so called manufacturers actually stopped selling to us because we were insisting on selling their vending machines at the fair market value and not the inflated prices encouraged by the Bus Ops.

This is not to say that there are no legitimate organizations that assist individuals with vending business opportunities. Certainly there are such organizations. The purpose of these examples is merely to educate you and better prepare you for the oldest scams known to the vending industry and make you alert to the possibilities of existing scams and also about scams that have not been thought of as yet! I continue to educate the general public in addition to vending business opportunity seekers. I share with them about the good, the bad and the ugly in our vending industry.

I take pleasure in consulting with individuals and vending corporations all over and am frequently astonished at the stories that are shared with me regarding the wide varieties of Bus-Ops operating all over our planet earth. There have been several national television broadcasts that have exposed vending scams in both rural areas and big cities throughout the USA and the world.

PIZZA MACHINE SCAM

One scam in particular that caught my attention was about a company that sold pizza machines as a business opportunity. They would offer to fly the prospect into their city and pick them up in a stretch limousine. They would proceed to wine and dine the prospect lavishly. This was all done after a substantial deposit was made and the prospect was being promised riches beyond their wildest dreams. The machines that were finally sold may have had a retail value of approximately $1500 to $2000 each. However, they were actually sold for $10,000 to $14,000 each and they would only sell lots of five or ten units at a time if the prospect qualified! Of course to qualify simply meant having a cashier's check ready and then they would promise that the prospect would have complete and exclusive control over a specific geographic area! The prospect (turned investor) would actually believe that they were now the proud owners of some exclusive vending program and ready to embark on their journey to riches and fame!

To make matters even worse, the prospects would have to buy the custom size pizza products from the seller's "presumed" bakery outlet and the pizza was not available anywhere else! To my amazement, the scam operation was able to deliver to some of the customers, but was unable to deliver to others and was not able to deliver on most of its promises, in spite of the tremendously incredible profit margin they were enjoying.

One or two investors who suspected that they were scammed began threatening to sue the organization. A few more called Hanna and a few other legitimate industry sources who later assisted them by recommending that they call on the District Attorney's office in their area to begin an investigation. Such pressure caused the Bus Op organization to close down immediately leaving hundreds of customers with instantly obsolete and less than credible vending equipment.

The saddest part of all these scam operations is the total devastation they cause the victims. These customers trusted the slick sales and marketing people and in many cases actually mortgaged their homes, lives and first born in order to buy into the dream that they were promised. While most scams may not be necessarily for big ticket items, they are just as demolishing to the smaller investors who may have only bought five, ten or twenty gum ball machines at inflated prices of $300 to $500 each when they could have purchased the same machines for as little $60 to $150 each.

BULK VENDING MACHINE SCAM

I remember a gentleman who called me in December of 1998 and he informed me that he had bought his first 10 units of "three selection" gum ball style vending machines from a source he believed might have been a scam operation. He thought that there was a possibility that he had over paid for the equipment and he had called some local vending companies in his area for advice and was finally referred to Hanna.

He explained that he had taken a cash advance on his charge cards in order to give himself and his wife a Christmas gift of a new "home business". However, he was later experiencing buyer's remorse. When he tried to call the people that sold him the vending machines they were not returning his calls. He discovered Hanna on line while he was browsing the Internet and ordered a copy of our catalog. When he received our Hanna catalog and learned of our every day low prices, he almost had a stroke! He was determined to grow his vending business and was relieved to find that we were not only a reputable company but that he was receiving all the consultation from us without any pre requisite for him to buy any equipment from Hanna whatsoever.

After some consultation with the gentleman, he informed me

that he was ready to buy more equipment from us and shared his financial status with me. I suggested that he consider getting a small bank loan or a lease and expand his business in the future by paying off his charge card debt and also adding that debt to his new purchase from Hanna. He was surprised that he would qualify for the loan with our assistance. He later discovered that he would easily qualify for the financing I arranged and he was able to buy three times the amount of vending equipment for the same investment he had given the scam operation.

It is the sincere satisfaction that such incidents bring to life for me that makes it all worthwhile. The good feeling I derive from seeing such success far exceeds the small dollar profits that we earn from any transaction.

COPY CAT SCAM CONSULTANTS

You should be alert to individuals and organizations that make reference to scams especially when the person making the claim has no established presence or strong track record within the industry. Some of these organizations will offer to share information with you in return for you to buy their equipment and will further offer exclusive contracts to insure that you will not be scammed! They may even mention names of individuals and organizations that will authenticate their legitimacy. You must be sure to follow up diligently in such matters. Even though Hanna has been consulting with new and also with established vendors for over twenty five years, it is important to note that when we offer consultation, we never expect to make a sale or receive compensation in return for the important information we share. Whenever we are asked to specifically consult with an individual or an organization in an extensive manner, we will occasionally negotiate a fee in advance for such services especially if it involves travel, review of intricate and extensive business plans or other time consuming and complicated issues. Since I have always been proud of Hanna being the leader in fielding calls on vending equipment sales, opportunities, scams and other related services, I have monitored the frequency with which "copy cat" operations attempt duplicating some of the services we offer.

I am extremely protective of the sound reputation that we have earned over all these years in vending and the acknowledgment we have received from the various vending and non-related vending businesses, government, media and civic organizations and others through out the USA and the world. I can honestly state that my objective is not to merely sell vending machines when appropriate but to educate the consumer and insure that a sound decision will be made, regardless.

NEW LEGISLATION ON BLUE SKY

There is on going progress being made regarding the prevention of vending scams. I am excited to share with you about the latest Blue Sky Legislation. This was added to SB 896 and passed by the Missouri Legislature. Governor Carnahan signed this into law on June 27, 2000 and it became effective August 28, 2000. Other legislation is being actively pursued and I anticipate similar legislation regarding other matters of importance to be passed throughout the United States and I will gladly make such news available in future updates of this book and in my newsletters and other sources of communication.

Chapter 8
PUBLIC RELATIONS

The general public usually knows very little about vending companies. Frankly speaking, this is due to the lack of interest on the part of vending companies to discuss their industry with the customer, the public and the press. We are viewed as a mysterious group of people in a serious and mysterious industry. Vendors rarely like to discuss their locations, sales, refunds, theft, vandalism, profit margins, commissions, security or whatever other details that are happening within their vending machine operations.

Customers who buy from the vending machines never believe there are legitimate reasons for price increases because most vending operators neglect to inform them about the frequency of price increases that the operators absorb along with all the other overhead cost factors that realistically affect the vending operation. Most people refer to the products in vending machines as "junk food" because few vendors are educating the consumers. This chapter was not intended to be a college course on public relations. My intention is to give you a quick insight as to some of the positive actions you can implement tomorrow morning in a simple and effective way.

Most vendors do not like sharing with the general public and others just do not have a clue on how to do so. We should not contribute to such a gloomy picture of the vending industry. It is not too difficult to make the customer aware of how good vending operators really are! You could easily discuss policies, menus, healthy selections, route drivers, styles and designs of vending machines and other interesting topics that customers are always asking about.

Hanna has been producing a "newsletter" for the past 25

years.

This is a tool to educate customers, creditors, government officials, employees, suppliers and other interested parties including the various news media. While this project takes up a significant amount of my personal time, I believe that it has been worth the effort.

Some vendors even use a simple one-page newsletter with information on one side of the page! The important thing to remember is that the consumer needs to know some of the basic news about the vendor serving them and the products and services that are available. If you anticipate a price increase, place a few sentences about the news you just learned. You should do this in advance of taking the price increase. By the time you are ready to approach your customer, they are already expecting the news and they understand why.

Newspapers, radio, television and other forms of media have been kind to Hanna over the years because of our willingness to share details of issues confronting our individual company and the vending industry itself. We have shared both the good and the damaging information about our industry, especially when we are allowed to shed new light on a subject that may have been misunderstood. You should consider doing the same.

Do not be afraid of the media, for they are only looking for news. If you are the one to genuinely share the news they are seeking, you will have a better opportunity to share the whole story, instead of them taking bits and pieces of a story and making public broadcasts that may be damaging to operators, manufacturers and distributors alike.

For example, some years ago, a man in the state of Kansas

was killed when a canned beverage vending machine from a vending company fell over and pinned him against the ground. The machine weighed more than one ton. The media had reported "MAN KILLED BY VENDING MACHINE" which did not make the vending industry look very good. It was a lazy Sunday afternoon when I received a message from one of the television stations asking me to return their call regarding this incident which occurred in a town approximately 40 miles away from our headquarters and where Hanna had no vending machines whatsoever. A handful of reporters had been calling vending companies all day and could not get anyone to return their calls to discuss how such a tragic vending machine fatality could occur.

When I learned of the telephone message from one of the reporters, I immediately returned his call. He wanted a company to explain how easily a canned beverage vending machine could fall over and kill someone. No wonder he was not getting his calls returned. Most of the vending operators and manufacturers were terrified of facing the media. They dreaded the thought of being placed in a compromising position to explain about how such an accident could have happened. No one wanted to be associated with such bad news.

My brother Michael and I discussed the request and immediately agreed to meet with their television crew at our warehouse that same Sunday afternoon to the reporter's surprising delight. Upon their arrival, my brother and I also decided that we would make sure that there would be no doubt that what we had to say would be communicated accurately to the general public. Therefore, we decided to literally sacrifice a vending machine to demonstrate the difficulty involved for an individual to cause a vending machine (exactly like the one in question) to fall over and kill a person accidentally! The reporter was thrilled and very appreciative that we chose to respond on such short notice and that we also agreed to voluntarily crash a perfectly good vending machine and not accept any payment for our time or property worth thousands of dollars. However, by the time we had demonstrated how much effort was needed and the tremendous difficulty involved to rock a large vending machine, much less have it fall over, the reporter was astonished. We invited him to assist us in rocking the machine while the camera was rolling and actually demonstrated "live" just how much effort it would take to crash the unit.

It soon became evident that a vending machine was not likely to accidentally fall over by itself, (as stated by the individual who made such claims) without a tremendous amount of intentional effort.

When we were done, we reminded the reporter that we had chosen to rock a vending machine that was totally empty and that if we had loaded the machine with 24 cases of canned beverages, it would have been significantly more difficult to move the machine! The result, they concluded, was that the machine was being vandalized severely by the victim and not a negligent act of a full service-vending operator, whose vending machine simply fell over and killed a person.

As it turned out, what could have been a barrage of bad press against vending companies became just another story of a bad guy becoming a victim of his own crime. While Hanna received no "Thank you" notes from any fellow vending companies, manufacturers, distributors or suppliers, my brother Michael and I had the personal satisfaction of doing our share of public relations and public service. We received calls from many customers who saw the effort that we made and were extremely warm and supportive of our efforts and our industry position. We impacted hundreds of thousands of people watching the news report, by making them better understand the serious consequences of rocking a vending machine to try and steal 50 cents worth of beverage product. Our local community appreciated our serious approach to correcting the public concern that vending machines were unsafe. The press did their job and was credible in their approach. As for Hanna...Was it all worth it? Would we do it again? Was it good for business? You bet.

There are other ways that you can provide a positive image in your hometown. One way is to get involved in civic organizational duties. Join a service organization like the local Rotary club, Chamber of Commerce, or any number of organizations and endeavors. By joining such organizations you may contribute to foster good will, create and improve friendships and share the truths that will be beneficial to all concerned. As a Rotarian for the past fifteen years, I try to uphold such noble and justifiable wisdom. You should also seriously consider doing this within the local community in which you live and work. After all, life should not consist of "all work" and "no play." Therefore try to combine play with your social duties. How great is that?

You could offer to give presentations about vending, its history, highlight opportunities for employment and many other interesting subjects that the general public would find very intriguing. I am always delighted to respond to requests to make short presentations to civic organizations, vending and related organizations and other entities on the vending industry. I am always amazed at the genuine interest that people seem to demonstrate regarding vending career opportunities, business opportunities, vending scams, new types of vending machines being introduced and other interesting and exciting vending details that are hardly discussed or explained to the general public. You can do the same too!

NOTES

Chapter 9

EQUIPMENT DEPRECIATION, ACCOUNTING AND TAX TIPS

The following brief information has been written for your benefit to explain the basic concept of depreciation. Please understand that this is only an introduction and not a complete or thorough guide to accounting procedures. I wanted you to have a brief understanding of depreciation and how it can work for you as an owner of equipment. It may be boring to some of you who prefer to depend on accounting specialists to handle such details but you should be aware of the basic principles. If you are like me you may not like to permanently bury your head in accounting details all day. However, if you are going to be in business for yourself, you must understand some of the basics or at least understand the importance of getting help to guide you as you grow . . . so here goes:

Anyone involved in a business that uses assets with a useful life of more than one year needs to understand the impact depreciation has on the income of the business both for tax purposes and from an economic standpoint. Depreciation is a term used to describe the decline in value that occurs as a result of using a fixed asset over a period of time. It is important to differentiate between depreciation for tax purposes and economic depreciation, which is sometimes referred to as "book depreciation".

Tax depreciation is calculated based on the rules described by the internal revenue code. The amount allowed as a deduction is calculated by multiplying the cost of the asset times the applicable rate. The rule is based on the life of the asset and the timing of the purchase of all fixed assets during the year. The rates may vary as the years pass by and therefore you may want to check with your CPA for a current table as it pertains to vending equipment. These tables may not relate to real estate or other assets that might be used in your business.

The internal revenue code also includes a provision known as accelerated depreciation, also known as Section 179 election. Under this provision a business is allowed to deduct a larger amount in the year the property is placed in service. The amount allowed is adjusted each year. I believe that as of December 31, 2000 the amounts per year were as follows:

$24,000 amount allowable for year 2001
$24,000 amount allowable for year 2002
$25,000 amount allowable for year 2003

The availability of this deduction is limited based on the income of the taxpayer. It should be noted that some portion of the deduction might be recaptured if the asset is not used in the business for a certain period of time.

Accelerated depreciation is a valuable tool to consider in reducing your income tax. If the business is operated as a sole proprietorship or a partnership it is important to consider the implications the election will have on self-employment tax as well as income tax.

The rules and strategies related to depreciation are complex and will have a significant effect on the economics of operating your business. It is strongly recommended that you seek the services of a tax advisor who is familiar with the intricacies of the depreciation system. Many Certified Public Accountants (CPAs) have received training in this area and other areas of business operations. CPAs are required to maintain their training by completing continuing education requirements each year. The use of a qualified CPA will be well worth the cost and will pay dividends in the long run.

Regardless of the amount deducted on your tax return it is important to consider the economic result of depreciation. If you only consider the tax depreciation of the current cash flow you might well come to the erroneous conclusion that your business is not profitable due to the tax losses or negative cash flows. You might also overestimate the profitability of the business. The economic cost of depreciation is best calculated using the straight-line method. Under a simplified version of this method you determine the expected life of an asset and then divide the cost by this number. For example if you have a machine that costs $5,000 and you estimate it will have a useful life of 8 years of 96 months the depreciation would be $5,000/96 or $52 per month. When you are evaluating the economics of your operation you need to reduce the income related to this machine by $52 per month to see your actual results of operations.

The interrelationship of tax and economic depreciation is an important and challenging concept. This is another reason why I strongly recommend that you retain the services of a qualified CPA to make sure you can see beyond the numbers to the actual results of operations.

TAX ADVANTAGES

There are other obvious advantages of starting your own business including numerous other tax benefits. If you start a small vending home business, you may be surprised about some of the immediate benefits for which you may qualify including legitimate tax relief on portions of your automobile, rent or mortgage payments, repairs, transportation and other expenses. These are matters for you to further discuss with your CPA. If you need more information or would like to know more about how to select a CPA near you, we will gladly share with you to the best of our abilities. Whatever you do, be sure that you maintain a credible and legal enterprise and comply with every aspect of law. You will soon discover that it is easier and safer than any other alternative.

HIRING YOUR SPOUSE & CHILDREN

There are tremendous tax benefits available to you when you hire your children and/or your spouse in your home business. If you have a parent or some other person living with you and you wish to hire them also, to help with some of the duties of running your small business. You may be surprised to learn that you could be eligible for many of the tax advantages that big businesses are already enjoying! Discuss these matters with your CPA and do not miss out on your numerous rights under the law. It is very exciting and you may even be able to save taxes that are currently being deducted from your current paycheck at your job... while starting up your business!

There are some more details in Chapter 12 on calculations you may want to consider regarding computation of sales and how to calculate your projected profits for a prospective account. If you were to contact The Hanna Group, additional info may be sent to you if you do not have a CPA.

IMPORTANT: Please remember that there are over 40,000 pages of tax regulations. No CPA is totally up to date on every intricate detail about these matters. There are a few experts that are known nationally for their expertise and up to the minute changes that could seriously affect you. Be sure that your CPA is truly on the cutting edge of the latest tax changes. Hundreds and sometimes thousands of pages of tax laws could change from year to year. I like to be in touch with the very best tax experts in the country when it comes to taxes. You can take advantage of these specialists too. If you should desire learning more about how to have all this plus **AUDIT PROTECTION** feel free to contact our offices and we will gladly share information with you. However, I would not want to mislead you into believing that we are accountants and tax preparers. We will merely guide you to additional sources whereby you may better educate yourself just like I did. The best professional advice is not as expensive as you may have thought! In fact you can actually purchase a comprehensive tax kit with all the detailed easy steps to follow. It will provide you with an organized, legal, moral and ethical format to follow without the use of a **CPA** if you prefer to handle your own details.

NOTES

Chapter 10

HOW TO GET NEW LOCATIONS MARKETING AND SALES STRATEGIES

There are countless ways to get new locations. This is one of my favorite and most exciting challenges. I cannot possibly go into all the details regarding all the sales and marketing techniques that one would learn from a formal business education on this subject. However, my objective is to offer some hard fast rules and popular strategies that are simple, creative and most importantly . . . EFFECTIVE! If you are a new vendor and you follow some of these simple strategies, you will be successful. If you are already in the vending business, you can certainly sharpen your skills by reviewing the strategies that are important and necessary. I have consulted with numerous major vending corporations over the years and am always delighted to meet members of their top management who were not ashamed to admit that they could always learn something new or refresh their memory regarding strategies that they had long since neglected to follow successfully.

These are by no means all the ways that you may gain exposure but you can get a quick idea of some of the most basic and effective methods that I have implemented over the years and which have proven to be very successful for me.

ADVERTISING & MARKETING

There are several ways to promote your enterprise. Some are more expensive than others, but not always necessarily more effective based on the costs. Here are some strategies for you to consider:

NEWSPAPER

Small ads can cost as little as little as $12 to $25 for large exposure in small towns and cities. You can also place larger ads that will attract even more attention. Many newspapers have a section for "Business Services." You will find plumbers, handymen/women, painters, electricians and other business services being advertised to introduce their availability. You can place small ads in these sections and ask for a special heading called "Vending Services." You may find yourself spending $50 to $100 for ads in big city newspapers but you should not start out spending big bucks till you have tested small ads in small papers.

FLYERS

These are by all means the lowest priced and one of the most cost-effective ways to get your message out. You would simply write a one-page message and include exactly what you are willing to offer. For example, 24 hours "fast and friendly" service, seven days per week 365 days per year efficient service, new or clean vending machines, national brand products, friendly personnel, no cost for the placement of the equipment, commissions available, office coffee service and other such items.

You may also want to mention the products that you are willing to offer such as Pepsi, Coke, national brand soda, juice, coffee, candy, chips, mints and whatever other items you have a desire to sell. Do not forget to insert your telephone in large bold type, after all, the whole object is to make sure that they find your number easily and call you immediately! This is your opportunity to give the prospect the necessary information to be motivated to pick up the phone and make that special call to receive more information. I have been very successful with this form of exposure.

YELLOW PAGES

This is one of the most powerful forms of advertising, but also one of the most costly depending on the size of the yellow page publication and the geographic area. It is a known fact that in most cases once a consumer has made the decision to make a purchase for any product or service they will immediately go to the yellow pages. This is the place that demonstrates for all practical purposes that you are probably a legitimate concern and that you are in business for the long haul.

Advertising may cost from as little as a few hundred dollars per year, to, as high as tens of thousands of dollars per year, depending on the size & color of the ad, city, art work and many other factors. You may want to start off keeping it small and choosing your words carefully. If possible, get some assistance from the yellow page representatives in your area because they can be most helpful. Once upon a time, I refused to use this form of advertising in a big way until I met a dynamite yellow page representative who took the time to educate me on the subject. I later expanded my ads from tiny one-line ads to the most dominant ads in each of the selected categories that I chose to advertise under. Yes, the results were just great! However it takes time, patience and money to select the right wording for the right services that you wish to provide. Start small...grow slowly!

BUSINESS CARDS

So many new business people underestimate the power of a business card. They do not need to be fancy or too wordy. Simply state your own name and a company name if applicable. You may include an address or post office box number and also one or more ways to contact you. You should include your home phone (Optional), business phone, cell phone, and fax number, e-mail address and at least one summarized line about what you do.

The line you use could be something as simple as, *"For all your vending machine needs."* Be generous with distribution of your business cards. Hand them out to everyone you meet and make sure that they know that you would appreciate their business. If they are not in a position to give you their business then ask for a reference to someone they may know who may need vending service. You would be surprised how many people you already know once you stop and think about it!

DIRECT MAIL

Once you have determined the types of business and the geographic area that you wish to target, you can easily acquire a mailing list from several sources. You would then send out a mailing to these business contacts with your message and possibly a brief letter of introduction. This would be the perfect opportunity to enclose that flyer (discussed earlier) that you would have already made and also your business card.

An effective enclosure would be a simple survey with about five or eight questions and offer to respond immediately if they send you the survey. You might ask questions such as: how many full time employees are at the location, how many shifts, are they happy with their current vending service, are they happy with their current selections of products, who is the person in charge of making decisions regarding their vending service, do they desire having more selections, do they have office coffee service at this time etc.

You would need to follow up with a phone call after you have mailed out your letters and surveys to insure that they received the information. Take this opportunity to try and get in and visit the location contact and offer to submit a "no obligation" proposal for their review.

VOICE MAIL

This is a very inexpensive way to share a brief message with those who are already calling you to get more information. State a brief message but also remind the caller of your product line, 24-hour prompt and efficient friendly service. Give your cell phone number for urgent or immediate response. This will portray a more professional image. You would not want this message to have a child's voice or a strange and crazy type of recording. I have contacted some vending companies that maintained a totally inappropriate recording with messages as follows:

"Here's the beep . . . you know what to do . . . do it!"

Or . . .

"I am busy right now, I will call you back if I feel like it . . . leave a message if you like."

Such messages demonstrate a lack of professionalism and will more likely scare away your prospects and customers than attract them! Some messages are recorded long before a business is started and the new business owner frequently forgets about the old recorded message. This can be a very costly mistake. I have also heard messages that sounded like a family recording and would have an inappropriate message as follows:

"Brad and I are out shopping and little Amanda cannot take a message as yet, so leave a message and we will call you soon."

While the above message may have been considered "cute"

prior to starting your business, it would be totally inappropriate once a business contact makes the effort to telephone your organization! Other messages portray a religious message or a Rock & Roll musical theme or the voice of all three children chiming in on what would otherwise be a totally charming recorded message. However, these types of messages do not offer an image of a serious business operation.

If you operate from your home, your friends and family should know that you have a business operation and they should expect a business recording if they call you. Your business contacts should not have to know that your office is in your bedroom or kitchen.

Your recording should be brief and business like. Preferably you should have a separate business phone line if you can afford to do so. You can also have some very inexpensive options as follows:

Call Forwarding: This will permit your incoming calls to follow you to your cell phone or other phones where you may be staying and you would be able to accept calls wherever you are.

Call Waiting: This option makes you aware of another incoming call which will enable you to put a personal or business caller on hold while you briefly take another call.

Caller ID: This is an excellent way to inspect the phone number of every caller who attempts to reach you including those who choose not to leave a message.

Live Answering Service: You can pay an organization to accept your calls 24 hours 365 days per year and then page you or fax you with the messages frequently. This service may cost more than the other above options but may be appropriate in some cases.

There are many other great options that your local telephone company can offer residents and small business people. Regardless of which options you decide to use, there is no excuse for not being as professional as possible even if you have only one telephone line.

There are countless examples of good recordings that may be used if you are using a recording message center. Here are few examples of messages that I believe may be acceptable:

"You have reached Hanna Vending. We are either on another line or temporarily away from the office and are unable to take your call personally at the moment. Kindly leave your name, telephone number and a brief message after the tone and we will respond immediately! If your call is urgent call Charles' cell phone # (***) *** ****. Here is the tone . . . "

Or. . .

"Thank you for calling The Hanna Group - For all your vending needs 24 hours, 365 days per year. We are sorry we missed your call and would like to return your call as quickly as possible. Would you please leave your name and telephone number after the tone? Thank you and have a great day! Here is the tone . . . "

You can improvise and customize your message with all the special details about your own operation.

VEHICLE SIGNS

While this is an inexpensive, easy and effective form of advertising, I have always felt hesitant to use it because of the

nature of our business. When people think vending machines they also, think cash . . . plenty of cash! Therefore, if you are in your vehicle and people know your every move, you must also consider the possible risks involved. Sometimes we choose to take some risk in exchange for the free or low-cost exposure.

For 25 years I never used this form of exposure in my local full service vending division. I also have never been exposed to robberies or serious incidents of theft from our vehicles. Many small and large vending companies choose to display their names and logos and even a picture of vending machines on their trucks.

There are no right or wrong ways. You decide for yourself!

DOOR TO DOOR

Never underestimate the power of a personal visit. I have been very successful with this form contact and of material distribution. It will take some effort but remember that it will only cost you your time. You can learn much from most receptionists who are usually anxious to share information especially if they are not happy with their current vending machine provider.

The visit should be very short and should be for the sole purpose of collecting basic but very important information while leaving some information for the main contact. Confirm the name of the main contact with whom you are going to communicate that day or at some time in the near future. Be sure that he or she is indeed the correct person assigned to make changes with their vending service. If you have already printed your business cards and flyers, these may be left behind at each location you visit regardless of whether you meet the contact person or not.

You may want to follow a simple script if you are not comfortable with new and creative introductions of yourself and your service. Here is a simple script that you may wish to consider as you hand the receptionist your business card:

"Hello, My name is Charles Hanna with Hanna Vending Service and I would like to speak with the person who is responsible for making decisions in reference to your vending machine service. Could you help me?"

Only two things can happen at this point.

1) The receptionist will call the person to visit with you and you WILL meet the contact person and most likely feel the thrill of instant gratification. Do not expect to land the account at this time. The only things that you are attempting to do is introduce yourself and gather information on the company and their needs and begin a rapport with the contact person. Do not expect to get this lucky too often however!

2) They will REFUSE to see you without an appointment and this is also just fine, as long as you gather all the information that is possible from the receptionist. Either way, you want to get the correct name, mailing address and telephone number of the contact in charge of vending and leave some introductory material for the contact to review. You may also wish to consider leaving a pack of gum or mints with the receptionist once you are done and ready to leave the location. The key to getting through to the contact in the future will be the receptionist! Treat that person with the utmost respect and they may remember you when you call back to set an appointment or speak with the contact.

Once you get back to your office, enter all the details on this prospect either on an index card or in your computer contact list, along with any relevant thoughts or ideas you may have about the location.

Remember to include the receptionist's name.
The receptionist will be your key to reaching your main contact in the future!

TELEPHONE MARKETING

I cannot begin to express how important and truly effective this manner of advertising communication has been for me. Some people are afraid to make phone calls or may not be capable of presenting themselves well on the phone. Once you have made the decision to detach yourself from the person you are calling you will be ready for the next big step. You must develop the attitude that you are going to make 50 calls and expect to generate maybe four or five good leads. This will insure that you will see some great results.

When I make calls, I am actually trying to get all the "No's" out of the way while remaining focused on the few "yes's" that I am seeking. I already know that there are companies out there who have bad service or no service at all. They probably have not heard from their vendor in forever! Your call may just be the most welcomed call about vending that they have had in days, weeks or months!

People are very attached to their "munchies" and when they are not able to get what they want when they want it . . . you become the answer they have been hoping for. Do not offer too much information unless they ask for more. Send out a package of information after the call and plan to follow up within a few days once again. The important thing to remember is that you must develop a phone script that is short and to the point especially if you are not comfortable improvising as you go along!

There are thousands of companies to call, therefore, do not be afraid to practice and also change the script as often as needed.

If you find a script that works well for you, keep it. Soon you will no longer need a script because you will begin to sound like the pro that you truly are. You may have already figured out by now that this is one of the least expensive yet extremely effective and immediate ways to promote whom you are and what you have to offer.

WEB SITE

Computer technology has revolutionized the way business will be conducted in the future. In fact, it has already made a significant impact on every business and consumer all over the USA, and practically the entire world. It is very affordable to create a web site and explain everything you have to offer. You can own and manage a web site for as little as $20 to $100 per year or less. There are even free sites available. This form of advertising requires much work and effort if it is to reach the audiencethat you desire and be effective.

Regardless, you may wish to include this aspect of sales and marketing in your arsenal and be prepared to communicate at the very least, via e-mail, along with all other inexpensive methods of communication that have now become commonplace in business.

To give you an idea of what we have done at our vending equipment sales web site, visit us at:
http://www.hanna-vending.com/

Since I also assist people by showing them how to invest wisely, save on their taxes, repair bad credit and other important aspects of personal and business enrichment, I have other web sites to specifically share the details.

Therefore if you are involved in more than just vending, you may be able to link the customers you have in one business to the web site of your other business. Many of my customers are involved in multiple businesses. For example, one such customer has been in the janitorial business and later decided to start a vending business. Slowly, but surely, he educated his customers about both of his businesses. Hence the customer asking for janitorial services would soon be asking him for a quote on his vending services and vice versa.

NOTES

Chapter 11

YOU ARE INVITED IN TO MEET THE MANAGER... NOW WHAT?

New vending machine operators panic at the thought of approaching new business prospects about vending. They shudder at the thought of confirming an appointment to review the account. However, I have known many new vendors who have called me from all over the country in a state of desperation and apprehension because they received a call from a business location manager expressing a willingness to meet with the new vendor to discuss their vending needs! What a wonderful problem to have! I usually smile when I get these calls because the vendor is obviously excited but wants to make sure that everything is going to be perfect.

There are no right or wrong ways to proceed when you receive one of these calls. What happens when a prospect agrees to meet with you while you are going door to door and decides that he is ready to listen to more of what you have to say while you are already at the front door! I will outline a few ideas for your review and the manner in which I would proceed if I were confronted with such good news.

Always have paper and pen in hand and ready to take notes when you walk in. Remember that list of questions on the survey sheet that I suggested you create and enclose with your mail outs? This is a great time to have that handy. If you are nervous, this is ideal for keeping you organized. You must take charge of the meeting at this time. You will be asking the questions and making notes of the answers. Do not be surprised if the prospect is also asking you questions. That is a good sign. It indicates their interest in possibly doing business with you. Listening is one of the most important secrets in sales! Never underestimate the power of listening!

Here are some of the things that you want to accomplish once you arrive at the location and have conducted the usual small talk about the weekend foot ball games, the weather and so on:

1) Inspect the vending machine area: You ask to inspect this area not to simply see the room or the decor but to determine the quality, type, style and model of vending machines currently at the location. You should be ready to make notes of the current variety and pricing of all products being vended without being obvious about this detail. However this will insure that you are able to at least match the pricing or in some instances reduce or increase the pricing, if necessary. Measure the space that will be available for your vending machines and inspect the number of electrical outlets if the machines you are placing are electronic and not manually operated.

2) Ask about their Office Coffee Service only if you have an interest in taking over that portion of the business also. Ask them how important commissions will be to the location. Most vending companies try to avoid this question. However if the prospect already receives a commission from their current vendor you will need to know this immediately. Remember that commissions may be determined by the selling prices of the products in the vending machines. The higher you set your selling prices, the higher the commissions you will be able to afford. Low prices may yield low to moderate or absolutely no commissions whatsoever!

3) It is important to determine how many full time employees and how many part time employees work at the location. Find out approximately how many visitors and other "walk through" traffic you may expect on a daily basis. Do they stay at the location during the days or do they travel? How many shifts are there? What are the hours worked on each shift? Do they work on weekends? Which holidays do they observe?

4) Determine how soon they may consider making a change of vendors if you can offer them everything they desire. How soon would they like to receive a proposal? Determine exactly what kind of problem they are experiencing with their current vendor. This is very important. You want to be sure that it is something you can improve upon immediately and make sure that you make a note for future reference now that you know how acutely they consider such a problem. You certainly do not want to give them reason to throw you out over the same reason shortly after you have invested in vending equipment and taken over the account!

5) Determine a time for the follow-up meeting, at which time you will bring the proposal and review it with the prospect. Once this date is determined, you may end the conversation with more small talk and get to know your prospect a little better. Find out about the prospect's kids, hobbies, skills and more about the company and possibly offer an invitation for lunch (on your expense of course!)

6) Send a "Thank you" note to the contact for taking time out of their busy schedule to meet with you and remind them that you are performing an account analysis and preparing a proposal for their review within a few days. I would like to suggest that you keep "Thank you" cards handy in order that you can mail them the same day that you visit the prospect.

7) An account analysis is nothing more than a quick calculation of the projected sales less the cost of goods, commissions and sales then tabulating your equipment cost in order to prepare a rough draft of a Performa. A Performa is your projected sales minus cost of goods and other expenses to give you an idea of your projected profit. This way you can determine what would happen if you actually bought equipment, installed the account and operated the account for approximately one year based on some simple but important numbers

that you have projected. To do this, you would want to determine exactly how many full time employees work at the company and multiply that number by an average of $3 to $5 of usage per week per employee. I like to use $4. Therefore if the account has 100 employees you would multiply 100 X $4 = $400 X 52 weeks per year = $20,800. Your cost of goods will vary depending on the volume of products you buy and how well you negotiate on your purchases. The selling prices of your products will also be an important factor. For purposes of this rapid calculation we will assume that you will sell most items in your vending machine for at least double the cost.

For example if you purchase your soda for approximately 25c per can you will sell it for approximately 50cents per can. For a quick estimate of your cost of goods you may want to use 50% until you have sharpened your skills and can tweak it more precisely. Among the expense items that you will obviously need to factor into the equation include: Sales tax, commissions to the account if applicable, labor costs, equipment depreciation, transportation expenses and so on. Once again, I will suggest a few estimated bottom line percentages that may be acceptable for you to consider. Your total cost of goods may be as high as 70% to 90% once you add up all your expenses. However you want to be careful not to end up with less than at least 10% to 15% profit. Your profit is nothing more than your projected income minus your expenses. Your CPA will be able to assist you with a customized format for you to follow. Unless you get involved with hot and cold food and frozen products, you may be delighted to learn that your profits will most likely be in the 15% to 25% bracket or better. Your return on investment will most likely be 25% to 100% or better.

8) After a careful analysis of the account, prepare a simple proposal outlining the vending machines you will place and the pricing of all the product categories and the amount of

commission to be paid if applicable. I personally prefer not using a contract. However many vendors use contracts and I believe that either way is fine with the exception that a contract can be intimidating

to the prospect. I prefer a simple letter format spelling out exactly what you intend to do for the prospect. Once you have prepared that proposal you are ready for the next step. Call and confirm your next appointment and be on time and be prepared to present the proposal and answer any questions the prospect may pose at that time. If you need more help with these matters call our company.

(9) Last but not least, ask for the business! I see so many vendors do everything stated above and submit the proposal...however, they never ask for the business! Do not make that mistake. The worst that can possibly happen is that the prospect decides to wait for a while. He may even decide to give his vendor one more chance to straighten up their act. Regardless, you are now in a much better position of getting the account very soon.

10) If you confirm the account, congratulations are in order. If not, do not take that to be a total defeat. Keep in touch with the contact by phone and mail. Send your brochure and business card at least once per month or every three months to remind the contact that you are still interested in the business. I have landed numerous accounts using this strategy after the prospect said "NO." Whatever happens, keep track of the details of communications on your index card or computer notes. This will become handy later! Frequently, the contact you discuss vending services with today may be gone tomorrow. The new contact will have no idea of your previous visit or communication with their company. By having the names and details of previous contacts and encounters you will be in a much better commanding position than the any other ven-

dor trying to solicit this account. Every one values their time and most location managers prefer to postpone tedious projects like these, especially when they have to start from scratch. Therefore if you can introduce yourself to the new prospect and announce that you already have all their details on file and that you would gladly submit a proposal at their convenience, you would definitely be the hero if they begin experiencing problems with their established vendor!

ACCOUNT RETENTION

Once you have successfully confirmed and placed the equipment on the account and begin servicing them regularly, one of the biggest mistakes you can make, is to ignore the customer. Do not assume that simply because you are serving the customer to the best of your ability it will insure your retention of the account. You must get to know your contact very well. Speak with them frequently (at least once per month or more if necessary but no less than quarterly) to insure that the customer is satisfied with the vending machines, products and services you are providing.

Keep the customer informed about new products, holiday schedule changes and other matters that will affect the quality of the service that is being offered. Set up a "refund fund" to insure that anyone who loses money in your vending machines can receive a refund promptly and courteously.

Respond to service calls as quickly as possible and maintain a log sheet of the calls and the type of problems experienced. This way you can share these matters with your customer if you are ever challenged about sloppy service. More importantly, you will be in a better position to justify replacing a certain vending machine or when you need to discuss the problems with your vending machine supplier who will demand such history of problems for a quick reference.

It is appropriate to invite your customer out to lunch occasionally and also to offer a few movie tickets or ball game tickets if your budget can handle such perks. It is not the size of the offer that matters but the very thought that you cared enough and remembered the customer that really counts!

If you can afford to special order small gift items like key chains and coffee mugs and similar items with your name and logo, telephone and address, do so. These are ways to keep your customers thinking about you and possibly referring you to more business in the future. These "give away" items are also perfect while visiting new prospects!

Regardless of how well you may believe your vending equipment, products and services may be, do not ever take the customer for granted. This is especially true when there is a change in location management and your "good friend," the location contact, resigns or leaves the company for whatever other reason, and you are now subject to review by the in coming "new kid on the block" who does not know who you are, and in most cases, does not care! In fact, new managers have a way of cleaning house for no-good reason whatsoever and that may include their current vending service! Therefore, you should be ready to move in and start your communication with the new contact and be prepared to treat the situation just like you did when you first landed the account. Remind the new contact how much you have enjoyed serving him or her in the past and that you look forward to working closely with them in the future to insure that every employee is totally satisfied.

Account retention is a process that never ends. It does not have to take hours or days of intensive effort to accomplish this duty within a small vending company. In fact, a few minutes, a quick occasional handshake, a phone call, a letter, fax, email or bulletins will suffice. A personal visit is always the most appropriate, if you can spare the time. No one can guarantee that you will have an account forever. However, I can assure you that many of the accounts that I served in my full service vending division for durations of five, ten, fifteen or twenty years, did not automatically decide to keep my services just because I expected it. None of those relationships were developed and maintained by accident. In some accounts, I had to deal with more than twenty contacts within the same organization over the years of serving them.

Frequently, there were multiple mergers and acquisitions with new owners, managers and employees. However, I remained focused on account retention. I cannot stress to you enough about this critical aspect of your duties as an owner or manager of a vending operation.

There are some important factors that will affect your bottom line and you may notice that I mention them more than once in this book. Some of these items include your cost of goods, payroll taxes, sales taxes, transportation expenses, machine maintenance, commissions paid to the location if applicable, employee benefits, spoilage, condiment expenses if applicable, general and administrative expenses, over & shortages, equipment depreciation and interest. However at this time I would like to highlight a few of which I believe are especially important.

SPOILAGE: When you work for yourself you will become very conscious of the amount of pastry and other similar items that may have a limited shelf life and therefore you will adjust your purchases and merchandising of these products to avoid as much spoilage as possible. You will be more attentive to these details because you are playing with your own money and you do not want to throw away your hard-earned dollars. However when you employ your first employee, it is easy to forget to monitor the losses from such spoilage. An employee is rarely as equally concerned as the owner of the business, therefore you must routinely be reviewing such matters closely.

SHORTAGES / OVERAGES: Once again, whenever you are buying your products, filling your own vending machines and collecting your own money, it is not as critical to monitor every collection with a sense of urgency. Keep in mind that it would still be a great practice in anticipation of hiring employees in the future! When you perform a simple calculation at each service and collection, you can determine if you collected the correct amount of cash in relation to amount of sales from the vending machine. For example, if you have a cold beverage vending machine that holds 200-12 oz. cans selling at 50 cents each, you would start out by filling the machine to its full capacity. Once you have done so, you would return a few days later to fill and collect the machine. If you find that the machine needs 24 cans to fill it back to the top, you would subtract the 24 cans from the original 200 and immediately determine that you should have 24 X 50 cents = $12 in the money pan.

If you only have $11 you can assume that there is $1 short or perhaps you gave a few refunds or a few free cans of beverages to customers or for yourself. Now you would at least know what happened! In some cases you may find $13 or $14 in the money pan and can assume that perhaps someone lost their money due to the fact that the machine may have malfunctioned! Either way, you would want to ideally receive the proper amount in the money pan at all times.

NOTES

Chapter 12
FINANCING - HOW WILL YOU GET IT?

There are numerous methods of financing for your vending machines, vehicles, inventory, warehouse and other needs. When I first started in vending in 1975, I had no money to buy vending machines. I was totally sold on the concept of vending and was hungry to get started. No one would finance me because I was new in the USA, had no credit background established and never worked for any company in America from whom I could secure a job or credit reference! I did not own a home and owned very little furnishings in my apartment. I had never borrowed money before in America and was simply not considered a good risk. How could I possibly get financing?

After I landed my first account and decided that I needed to buy my first vending machine I panicked when the bank said NO! The customer was waiting for the machine and I was desperate to oblige. With a stroke of luck, I discovered a solution (listed below) and immediately went to work implementing my plan of action.

There are numerous sources of financing available. This overview is not intended to give you every aspect of financing details, but is merely an attempt to open your eyes to the possibilities and some of the choices you may wish to consider.

FAMILY - FRIENDS - NEIGHBORS

Most people underestimate the combined financial power of their family, friends and neighbors. I refer to these sources as "Angels." When I first started business in America, it occurred to me that I had very few friends, couple new relatives in Kansas City, and I hardly knew my neighbors.

However, as the years rolled by, I learned the secret of successfully tapping into these sources for financing.

I would prepare a plan of action by outlining exactly what I wanted to purchase, the cost of the items, the manner in which I would sell it at a profit, outline the amount of profit and an example of how much interest I was willing to pay for the use of the money to do all of the above. If I really needed $1000 and one of my friends had only $400 I would discuss the same plan as I would with one who had $600 or the total of $1000. I would explain everything and lay all my cards on the table honestly.

Once I borrowed the money, I would immediately begin some repayment program making small payments weekly or monthly in order to show good faith. I would include the interest and give updates regarding the progress and development I was making and just how helpful the money had been for my small growth. This impressed my handful of Angels whom I had very carefully selected to approach on the subject. This was due to the sensitive issue of doing business with such individuals who were close to my heart. Once again, before long, they would be coming to me asking how much more I would be needing to borrow because they really enjoyed doing business with me . . . not to mention the fact that the interest I was willing to pay was not too shabby either. I borrowed money at 10% to 15%, which was lower than any other interest for which I would qualify at the time. Yet, this was more than double or triple what they were making in their savings accounts, or worse, sitting in their checking accounts. Soon, I was borrowing $1000 to $5000 from individuals, and my business began growing rapidly.

CHARGE CARDS

While this is not the smartest way to borrow money, it is no doubt the easiest way to get instant credit. Most people who use charge cards usually buy luxury items, dinners, vacations and other expenditures that do not make money. However, if a person understands how to borrow $100 and buy a product and sell it for $200, then everything changes! I discovered that I could not only buy a vending machine, but more important, I could buy products and double the price of the products rapidly and pay off my original amount borrowed.

It did not matter to me at first that I was paying 14% to 20% interest. Soon, the charge card companies were extending more and more credit to me, and I began to shop for more competitive charge card rates. Before long, my banker began to notice the size of my deposits from sales collected from my vending machine placements. When I explained to my banker what I was doing for financing, he called me into his office and said that it was time for us to chat again! Once he saw that I was handling the cash in a responsible manner, he was finally encouraged to take a chance on me. I soon qualified for my first bank loan, which leads me to my third source of financing.

BANK LOANS

These loans range from small car loans and consolidation loans to major loans that include home mortgages and business consolidations. My first loan was very exciting. I managed to borrow enough to pay off all my charge cards and the handful of family, friends and neighbors immediately. I then had only one large loan with a lower monthly payment and interest fee than all the previous activity combined. The bank now held a first position on all my vending machines including the very breath I inhaled!

Once I accomplished this feat, it was amazing how things started to open up for me. Suddenly, charge card companies were sending me pre-approved charge cards with $5,000 and $10,000 limits. Friends and family were excited to see the growth and they were standing in line to help in any way that I was bold enough to ask for! In fact, not too long after these brief measures of success, my brother Michael and I decided to become business partners. We soon joined forces not only financially, but brought every ounce of our individual and unique gifts to the table. It was this combination of strengths and strategies that made it possible for us to continue moving forward, later building a major corporation. Understanding the basic bank loan strategy is very important if you are to become truly successful. Banks want to lend money to responsible people. If you can demonstrate responsibility and the ability to perform consistently, they will love you. If you fail to live up to these measures, they can crucify you.

Once you are able to walk into any bank and request a loan and get it, you will wonder why you ever went to family, friends, neighbors or your friendly charge card companies! However, do not ever hang up those other sources of financing because you must always remember that always need Angels who are waiting to come to your rescue . . . just in case! :)

SBA AND OTHER GOVERNMENT LOANS

If you can qualify for certain types of loans, you would be surprised at the significant differences each can contribute. I remember my first Small Business Administration (SBA) loan very well. I had borrowed all I could from my banker and was growing rapidly. However, my banker was beginning to get uncomfortable with the speed of the growth. One thing you must understand about bankers is that they are overly cautious and conservative and for the most part, skeptical! When they would not comply with my requests as swiftly as I thought they should, I rediscovered my "Angels" who were wondering what took me so long!

Once I began to feel the pressure of the fast growth and the need for additional financing, I realized that I needed to investigate further options. I soon met another banker while attending a Chamber of Commerce luncheon. Since he asked me about my business, I decided to explain my circumstances briefly and asked his opinion about all the options that were available to small business people like me.

I learned that the SBA was the next step. While I was preparing and studying everything about the SBA requirements and all the pain staking procedures that were necessary to fund my growing operation, my Angels came to the rescue to keep me operational and growing. This time I negotiated short term financing with my Angels at slightly reduced interest rates but still very lucrative financing terms for them.

The government-sponsored loan packages usually guarantee a certain percentage of the loans that are being negotiated and allow the banker to make the loan while taking less risk at their bank. BINGO! Even though I was no financial genius, it made sense to me. Uncle Sam wants business to prosper in America and understands that risk is inevitable. The government also understands the psychological and economical make up of the average banker. Bankers simply do not like to take any unnecessary risks whatsoever. They are not motivated to be "nice guys." However if the government is to stimulate the economy and help create jobs and further the insurance of stability and robust economic conditions at a city, state and federal level, then it must help business people with a helping hand to grow and prosper.

This is a key factor in the USA economy. It has been implemented and proven to be more successful here than anywhere else in the world. With some coaching from my new banker, the accumulation of relevant data and financial documents, I successfully secured my first SBA loan...so can you!

Soon I was able to take my previous bank loan, all my credit cards, and other small loans including the debt on my growing fleet of business vehicles and combine them into one large government-guaranteed loan with a special lower interest rate and even lower monthly payment than before!

I was also able to include some new equipment that I wanted to buy and also build my product inventory for new projected growth . . . and grow we did! I actually went on to negotiate numerous other successful SBA loans over the years that followed.

Do not be afraid to visit your banker (loan officer) and ask about these and other government guaranteed loan options. There are even special privileges for minorities such as Women, Hispanics, Asians and African Americans to name a few. Do not be discouraged if your banker says "NO". In fact do not be discouraged if you have a less than desirable credit rating. I will gladly share with you how you can eliminate such handicaps legally and morally. Many individuals allow a divorce, bankruptcy, delinquent school loans and other blemishes on their credit to dampen their enthusiasm for growing a business. I want to share with you options that will place a smile on your face.

LEASING

There are many different ways to enjoy the use of vehicles or vending and related equipment on a lease program in the same way you would if you bought them. Basically, a lease allows you to take possession of the items you desire without having to purchase them and place them on your books as an asset.

A lease may not always be the least expensive way to borrow money, but it may be an excellent way to write off the purchase from a tax perspective. Leases may be structured for as short as a six-month period to approximately sixty months. I will attempt to super simplify the general idea behind the leasing options but these are by no means an in depth education. My intention is to give you a quick and simple translation of this type of financing, as I understood it. I am sure that you will be able to discuss these matters with a leasing company or your friendly banker and get a much more accurate description of all the additional details involved. Here goes . . .

Some lease contracts allow you to purchase the equipment at the end of the term of the lease for just $1.00. Ordinarily, you would use the equipment for the full duration of the lease and at the end of the lease you may decide to let the lease company take back the equipment and you may simply get new equipment and start a new lease. You may wish to refer to this type of lease as a "One Dollar Buy Back." You would use the equipment exactly as though you own it. However, you must always remember that you do not own it until you have exercised your option to do so. At the end of the term of the lease, if you do not buy the items that were leased to you, then you have the right to "Walk Away" and not own the items toward which you had made lease payments over the preceding months and years.

There are opportunities for you to lease the same items for usually a lower payment than the "One Dollar Buy Back lease." These leases may sometimes be referred to as a "10% Buy Back Lease." At the end of the lease, you are allowed the option to buy the items for 10% of the original price that was negotiated on the items leased. Everything is negotiable as far as the original structure of the deal. You may wish to discuss whatever percentage of a "buy back", you desire such as a "12% Buy Back Lease" or a "15% Buy Back Lease" etc.

Therefore, at the end of any such lease you would pay a higher price for the purchase of the items because every month of the lease you were paying a lower payment than the "One Dollar Buy Back" program.

Many companies that buy computers, for example, may exercise their option at the end of this type of lease to "Walk Away" and initiate a new lease for the latest computer technology on the market. Other companies may choose to keep the older equipment and upgrade the computer boards and similar options and find the "10% Buy back" option to be just right! Of course they would have the option of paying the agreed percentage amount to purchase the equipment or at the last moment decide to Walk Away" or "Abandon" the lease that is sometimes referred to as an "Abandonment Lease."

Another popular lease is known as "The Market Value Lease." In this scenario, you would lease the same equipment but very possibly pay an even lower monthly lease payment than the "10% Buy Back Lease." At the end of the lease you would have the option of purchasing the equipment at the current market value that may be determined by the lease company.

Once again, computers are an excellent example of the type of equipment that would be ordinarily best suited for this type of leasing program, especially if you have determined that you would more than likely want to "Walk Away" from this type of equipment within one or two years anyway! This is because the values of such equipment that has rapid technological advancements tend to become obsolete over a short period of time.

There is much to learn about leases. Once you decide to enter into a lease, you should familiarize yourself with the specific program that you believe would be most advantageous to you in the long term, both from a tax and ownership perspective. Your local friendly banker may be a good source for some education on the subject or you may find a local reputable leasing company to discuss your specific needs and the programs they may wish to recommend for your consideration.

On a final note, you may wish to consider that in some cases, when you may not qualify for a regular bank loan or government loan, leases may be just the answers, or frequently, the only answer! There is no specific way to calculate a percentage of interest because leasing companies do not use an interest rate when you lease. They use "Factors." For example you may purchase $10,000 worth of vending machines on a 60-month Abandonment Lease with a factor of .0252. You would multiply the $10,000 by .0256 and you will have a monthly lease payment of approximately $252. Remember, this is only an example and the "factors" that are used varies and so does the payments.

These "factors" are frequently determined by the strength of your credit rating. Leases are sometimes an easier source of financing for which you may qualify, since you do not add the items purchased as an asset on your books. The items that are leased are also not up for grabs by other creditors who may zoom in on your assets in the event that your business should fail. The leased item remains the property of the organization that has granted you the lease. I know . . . I know . . . I know . . . it is a little confusing and I personally still struggle with the decision of which lease is the best lease or whether I should lease or not lease, depending on the transaction. Decisions, decisions, and more decisions. You wanted options? These were just a few!

OTHER SOURCES OF FINANCING

There are major insurance companies that are capable of structuring extremely large financing projects because they are not as tightly regulated as some regular financing institutions. Taking on active or silent partners can also be a way to generate new money, not to mention brain and labor power to boot! Some companies decide to sell shares in their companies and others go public and find it possible to access large sums of money to grow their organizations. Sometimes creative financing can be overlooked. Some examples may be as simple as trading your car to someone in exchange for the vending machine they want to sell. Some individuals have been known to offer a piece of land or a lake home that they no longer use as a deposit or total payment for a group of vending machines or a route that is for sale. This allows the buyer of the vending equipment to by pass the traditional borrowing of funds for the acquisition and use a piece of property that may not have sold for as high a price as the value of the vending equipment that they wanted to buy!

The important thing to remember is that whether you are a "mom & pop" operation or a multi million-dollar corporation, you will need financing to grow. How you go about finding this money is most important if you are to be successful.

Chapter 13
HOW MUCH SHOULD YOU PAY FOR A VENDING BUSINESS?

It should come as no surprise to you that there is really no magic formula to arrive at a price to pay for any business. This is because no two businesses are ever exactly alike and the vending industry is no exception. Demand and supply determines the value just like it does in any other business. However, there are some basic principles and strategies that you can follow if you are ready to buy or sell a vending business. I have personally helped hundreds of individuals over the years to start their own vending companies successfully using some basic strategies.

The quality of the equipment and the volume of sales may help to determine the value of the vending route you will buy. If you buy mechanical equipment versus electronic equipment, the price will naturally be lower. Since the vending equipment is already on location and generating revenue, it should be considered more valuable than sitting in a person's garage. In some cases it may be considered even more valuable if the seller is prepared to assist you and train you plus back and support you for some duration of time after the sale.

Some sellers also may have the ability to sell you the products for the vending machines at wholesale. They may even stock the parts for repairs and also offer service calls as an option. The more that you can get from the seller in the way of assurances, training and guarantees, the more valuable the route will become. In many cases when a major deal is being negotiated, it is common for the buyer to offer the seller a key position in the company if the seller would agree to stay on for a specific period of time. In fact, this strategy is crucial to the successful negotiations, which will help lead to the final conclusion in many transactions.

If a route generates approximately $50,000 in gross sales per year, you may expect to pay approximately $25,000 for your cost of goods. That leaves you with approximately $25,000 to pay your salary, fuel costs, sales taxes, parts, repairs, rent (if applicable) and other expenses.

Some sellers attempt to receive as much as two or three times the gross sales from a route when they decide to sell the route. They will ask $100,000 to $150,000 for the $50,000 that I just mentioned. If you were to actually buy that route for such a price, it would be due solely to your lack of proper investigation and also due to your ignorance on the subject of vending route values.

A route that generates $50,000 annually may fetch as much as approximately $50,000 if the seller is prepared to offer much back-up and support long after the sale. I have helped many vendors to start out this way and helped them for many years after they bought a small route. I would assist them in numerous ways that an average seller would never ordinarily consider. However, my customers would always return and purchase more vending machines and related equipment as the years rolled by and they would also buy the snack and beverage products from our wholesale division.

We would even assist them with their proposals when they were working on new accounts and we would also help them with leads for new vending locations. In many cases we could have easily charged much more than $60,000 or $70,000 for the same $50,000 in annual sales. Why? Because we offered much more value before, during and long after the sale than anyone else would ordinarily want to do. What I did was not the norm in the industry. However the reason I had chosen to share that particular expensive option was to make you aware of the other extremes, whereby genuine value may enhance any transaction.

Small routes generating $25,000 to a few hundred thousand dollars may not need much complicated contractual agreements if every one is a pro and understand the consequences of the pending deal. However, if you are not experienced, you may need all the help you can get. Either way, in a small transaction you will learn quickly and should not be exposed to any significant losses if you now understand some of the basic information I have shared with you.

If you are buying a route and you are prepared take some more risk and be diligent regarding the investigation of most of the details regarding the transaction, you may be able to pay less for the route. You will have the opportunity of visiting the accounts and investigating the income to make sure that the sales are actually legitimate and not just a promise from the seller. You may not need as much security and guarantees from the seller. Your comfort level may be such that you will not need to have someone hold your hands through the transaction for weeks, months or years after the sale. The deal is very straightforward. That is why you will expect to pay less for the route. You may even be in a good bargaining position because the seller is motivated to sell and you are now going to offer to make his deal very easy to conclude. This could mean that the purchase price may now drop to $25,000 or lower for the same $50,000 annual sales on that route.

If the route is distressed, customers are complaining, machines are empty or old and dirty and the general appearance of the over all operation is simply not appealing, the price just dropped even further! You are about to take on even more risk. It is not unusual to pay as little as $8,000 or $10,000 or less for the same size route when the risk is increased. By the time you take over a distressed route, you may easily lose 50% of your accounts before you have a chance to correct the problems to the satisfaction of the location managers.

The vending machines have a certain value regardless of the volume of sales. For example, $50,000 in gross sales may be generated by as little as four or five machines or as many as 50 or more machines. These could be little gumball machines or large soda and snack vending machines. It may depend on the location and the quality of vending machines, number of employees at the locations, number of shifts at each location and the days of the week that they are open for business. For the purposes of this example, assume that the route has 50 machines. All machines are older canned beverage vending machines. I have sold very old canned beverage vending machines from as little as $25 or $50 each. Others have sold for as much as $600 or $1000 or in excess of $3000, depending on whether they were re manufactured with new dollar bill acceptors, coin mechanisms, with warranties, back up, support after the sale, brand new "state of the art" equipment etc ... etc ...

Once you determine that a machine is only worth for example $300 in "as is" condition, then you start analyzing from that point. You must ask yourself several more questions, such as: What happens if I lose the account? Will I be able to sell the vending machine? If so, how much will I get? As unlikely as it may be, what happens if I lose all my accounts? Will I be able to at least break even by getting back close to what I initially paid for the route? By using this example for illustration purposes, you can calculate that the above route doing $50,000 annually with 50 machines at a value of approximately $300 each would be worth $15,000 in a worst-case scenario!

If the market prices of the vending machines come close to the total price you decide to pay for the route then you are in good shape. You also have to factor in the price of other equipment such as vehicles, coin counting equipment, furniture and similar items if applicable. However in matters of very small routes, these factors do not come into play! There is some value to the established route sales that is already being generated. You may choose to add a little more to the asking price of the route for that income or not. This is all negotiable. Occasionally, the seller is willing to stay on and help run the route with you as part of the deal. This can also enhance the value of the sale. If the seller is willing to finance a portion of the deal that is the best scenario! Why? Because if he is willing to take a risk to sell his route and wait for a portion of his money, he must be also confident that everything he has shared with you is absolutely true and verifiable. However, most people who want to sell are doing so because they need the cash to do something else! You must make every effort to insure that the deal is genuine.

Some opportunities may involve very large routes or an entire corporation for sale. Sometimes it may be only a division of a large vending company that is for sale and not the entire organization. You are more likely to encounter individuals with very small routes for sale and not the multi-million dollar deals. When my brother and I decided to sell our multi million-dollar local full service vending division, we never advertised our routes anywhere! After a careful study of the qualified candidates, I simply made one phone call to an organization that I thought was credible, ready, willing and able to handle the size of our full service vending division. We reached a mutually acceptable price. The deal was successfully completed in a very short period of time. I agreed to stay on with the organization until they were comfortable enough to handle the daily routine on their own. During that time, I was able to maintain my other vending and business enterprises successfully.

SOME MORE EXAMPLES OF SMALL DEALS

If you were to notice for example, an elderly lady, who advertises a vending route for sale, you may find it quite believable that she is offering a genuine opportunity. This would be especially true if after some investigation you were to determine that her husband just passed away and she does not have the slightest idea of what to do about the route that he was running for the past many years. This would be a genuine example of nothing that would resemble a scam!

Sometimes a couple gets a divorce and the court determines that their vending route must be sold and the proceeds split between the couple. Such scenarios may be genuine situations where a route may become available for sale. However, there are numerous other genuine occasions for you to find a good vending investment opportunity. You may wish to pursue individuals who are just ready to give up their vending route and try something else or simply cannot maintain the route plus their existing job any longer! Health issues are another set of reasons that create genuine opportunities when looking at routes for sale!

As I mentioned before, when negotiating price, some of the other bargaining chips may include the route vehicle, parts, inventory of goods in the vending machines and in storage. You must consider office furnishings including computer and software and other such items that may be negotiable or just bundled together as one large package deal for the same price of the value of the vending machines.

The most important thing to remember as you are reviewing the deal is that it may still be a scam! The person may have just started in business and is offering you what appears to be a well-established business, when in fact; he just started a few weeks ago or a few months ago! Therefore, ask plenty of questions if you are not sure. Some of the questions that you may wish to ask could be as follows: Where do you buy your supplies? How long have you been buying there? How well do the management and staff know you there? May I ask them about you? What are the best-selling items in your machines? May I see your deposit slips that prove the amounts that are being collected from your machines? May I chat with your banker to get a reference on you? May I see your last year's tax returns? If a person is hesitant to chat freely and openly with you… that should be your clue to advance with extreme caution!

Finally, do not confuse buying a business from a genuine vendor who is selling his established route for legitimate reasons with that of a scam artist. They can sometimes resemble each other. Keep in mind that a scam operation will hastily build a route to sell you with little regard for stability of the account and will not share with you that they are doing so. If an organization promises to sell you a route that they are currently building rapidly just for resale, it is ok to buy from that individual if she has shared all the details with you in advance. You should also realize that you are increasing your level of risk because there is no established relationship between you and the vendor or the location.

Therefore, you must fully understand that there are individuals who go out and find locations, service them for a short while and then advertise the route for sale. The problem with this strategy as I just explained is that there is no solid relationship between the vendor and the location management. Usually, the vendor is building this route in order to quickly sell it and may not usually care what happens to you in the long term!

There are many more ways to possibly structure a sale of a route. This short overview could not possibly cover all of the ways necessary for every case scenario. However, by understanding the over all idea of spotting a genuine business opportunity from that of a scam, your chances of success will increase tremendously! Do not be afraid to get some professional help. In some cases, if you are buying a vending route from a business broker, you will find that you may depend on a built-in professional as a source of added protection for you the buyer. Keep in mind that the broker may not be knowledgeable about vending or the vending industry! Hanna will gladly discuss specific circumstances with you should you desire.

Chapter 14
WORKING FOR AN EXISTING VENDING COMPANY

You may wish to consider working for a vending company, prior to starting your own. This may be especially helpful if you are serious about building a sizeable company and want to have first hand experience without investing any of your own money! Often, individuals or vending corporations buy out other vending companies or divisions of other vending companies and maintain most of the existing management and staff. If you already work for a vending company and are thinking of owning your own vending operation, you may already have a good idea of how everything should work. If you are unsure of yourself, you may want to apply for work at a vending company to get some experience. If you are serious about learning about the industry and the daily tricks of the trade, this is an excellent strategy. Large vending companies operate slightly different to smaller ones. There are endless combinations of personalities, educational background and vending experience that management and staff of vending companies have. I will share only a few examples of how these may affect you depending on the circumstances that you may face. However do not allow these facts to discourage you from owning your small vending operation.

NEW OWNERS

Whenever there are new owners of a company or in the case of a merger, they bring their own style of operation that may be slightly or totally different to the style of the existing management. Sometimes the new owners become actively involved at the company on a daily basis and have direct and frequent contact with the employees. In some cases the new owners are simply acquiring a new division that may be added to a long list of other divisions all over the state or all over the country for that matter and you will rarely see or hear from the owners directly! Instead, you will interact with the managers assigned to that division in conjunction with top ranking management members such regional managers, regional vice presidents, executive vice presidents, working co owners and other similar members of management. Some owners negotiate with the existing management and staff of a newly acquired company (Which may include previous owners of the company that sold out) to stay on and everyone soon discover just how compatible the existing combination of new management and staff will be.

Small acquisitions may not be as complicated. These may include a small vending company with annual gross sales of $50,000 to approximately $300,000. Usually, the new owner takes over the small route from another small vendor owner and after some training from the previous owner; they will handle all the day-to-day business details on a personal level. Sometimes the existing owner is ready for retirement and he will offer the route to an existing route driver or supervisor if there was an interest. Otherwise, they will find an interested party to buy the route via advertising.

Larger acquisitions tend to be more complicated. Existing employees of the company that is being sold are more likely to jump ship and pursue some other interests or move to another vending company because they are unsure of the new management who may possibly create too many changes beyond their comfort level. If the new owners are intelligent, educated and experienced vendors, they will already know how to treat people fairly and with respect and appreciation. It always amazes me to learn of the major hardships that confront new owners in major acquisitions. They are sometimes not ready to change with the times or maybe some of their senior members of their management team are simply not qualified academically or emotionally to manage with compassion, understanding, fairness and in an unbiased manner. In short, some of these managers are considered dinosaurs of another era. They have experience in some aspects of vending but lack the people skills to maintain stability within the newly acquired company. In my experience over all the years that I have been in the vending business, I have always been amazed at the lack of professionalism in certain senior management members. In most cases these individuals have not necessarily worked their way up in the organization and earned their positions based on all the criteria necessary to successfully manage effectively. These individuals are sometimes family members who have assumed high ranking positions by default or had become friends with the owners at some point and later negotiated their positions due to long standing relationships without regard for the necessary credentials to actually perform the job properly. Thus as the company grows, there is a false sense of security on the part of the owners, due to the fact that the owners either refuse to recognize such realities or they themselves are also not qualified to recognize those who are most qualified for the job. Instead, they bury their heads in the financial details of the organization and forget the most important assets within their organization.... their loyal and qualified management and staff. If a survey were to be taken of most major vending companies or any large corporation, one would quickly discover the frustration that is being experienced by very qualified members of the organizations who eventually become disenchanted by the indifference shown by the very top ranking managers including the owners of the organizations toward their very capable and qualified existing middle and upper management and staff.

Therefore, do not be discouraged if you work for a vending company and discover that there is significant disparity among the corporate family, management and staff members.

Your priority is to learn the fundamental procedures of the operation and to recognize how you may handle them even better if you owned the company. I would like to suggest that you owe it to the owners of the organization to communicate your suggestions freely and clearly in order that they may have every opportunity to take corrective action.

There are some owners or top levels of management who respect and appreciate communication, especially if it relates to less than desirable policies that may not be effective or worthy.

MANAGEMENT BY INTIMIDATION

A clear indication of a manager, who is not capable of managing effectively, is one who uses intimidation techniques to frighten his subordinates into submission. The use of unnecessary secrecy and micro managing techniques become extremely frustrating to good workers who may not tolerate such obvious sub standard managerial behavior for very long. It is important for you to understand that such poor performing, high-ranking managers are hesitant to relinquish control and refuse to truly empower their key employees and middle management team members. Many of the middle and upper management figures who report to such high ranking managers are frequently surprised to learn that they are more qualified for the high ranking job than the person to whom they are reporting! I am frequently baffled at the fact that the owners of such organizations who empowered those high ranking individuals, are usually unaware of the loose canons they have selected to represent them in such a high positions. Frequently, the owners rarely hear the truth from the lower ranking management team regarding the severe lack of tact in such high-ranking managers. This is often due to the fear that has been instilled across the board by some high-ranking managers who usually enjoy wielding the power that was granted to them by the owners or top management of the company. You may even have to learn to let ugly comments run off your back like water off a duck.

The owners of such companies are usually too busy to notice the negative effects their choice in management is slowly causing the company. As long as there is growth and some profitability, most owners are willing to bury their heads in the sand. No one is willing to rock the boat and most middle management members and some top-level managers frequently give in to being "yes men" rather than speaking their mind genuinely and directly to the owners or board members. Having an open door policy is not enough if an owner does not enforce it and also allow every employee to communicate outside of a threatening environment without the fear of losing one's jobs. Therefore, proceed with caution and learn all you can from free "on the job training" and remember that you are being compensated to boot!

PROFESSIONAL OWNERS AND MANAGERS

Educated, experienced, credible and liberal owners recognize these issues. They are usually receptive to the idea of positive traits and frequently use basic skills such as listening, reading, and discussing issues openly and honestly. It is most important for them to appreciate the courage that it takes for individuals within an organization to step forward and bring important details to the surface. Stepping forward is difficult with the possible threat of the looming dinosaurs that are an ever-present hindrance to the very same organization by default. Owners of successful organizations do not have a need to be envious or jealous of their most promising management and staff members. To the contrary, they will usually be encouraging, understanding and patient. They will have the capability to recognize quality over quantity and appreciate a genuine and open discussion with their managers even if the opinions expressed are not always exactly in line with their own. These owners will demonstrate a genuine respect and frequent gestures of appreciation for efforts that are reasonably well delivered by their managers in the best interest of the organization. If you desire working for a large vending company, you should seek out an organization with owners or a board of directors who display such solid qualities and then hope that the rest of the upper management in the organization is committed to a similar philosophy.

When you do make it to the top of such an organization, you will have the unique opportunity to make a distinct and positive difference. Whatever you do, try to never get caught up in the petty politics of the organization to any substantial degree. Do not choose to participate in the distracting and unprofessional behaviors that may drag you down to the levels of others. Rise above it all!

RUMORS, LIES, JEALOUSLY & GREED

I have learned some extremely valuable lessons in both my personal and business career that I would ordinarily not share with the average person with whom I come in contact. However, it is important that you understand some of the fundamental truths that I believe are harsh realities.

RUMORS

I have always believed that if I can stop a rumor within my own company I would do so immediately by sharing candidly with my management and staff whatever information I believe is true and constructive. I am convinced that it is better to prevent a rumor than to correct one. In the event that a rumor has started, I usually waste very little time in responding therefore preventing it from festering among the employees. An example of this situation was 1992 when one of our competitors started a rumor that Hanna was getting ready to lay off many employees. After several loyal employees confidentially approached me as to whether they should be looking for another job, I immediately called a meeting of all Hanna employees. I explained that I had heard the rumor, and as always, I would be candid with everyone to the best of my ability. I went on to express that the rumor was nothing more than a lame trick our competitors were using to cause dissent among our management and staff because of the fear they had regarding the expansion efforts Hanna was getting ready to undertake! This in turn would hurt our competition severely and I explained that I needed everyone's support more than ever before and that I would actually give a bonus or finders fee to anyone who would refer qualified prospects to Hanna for employment. This seemed to resolve the problem immediately.

Another rumor in the mid 80's was that Hanna was having severe financial problems and would go bankrupt within a few months. We actually lost a few employees before I learned of the rumor! As always, I called a meeting of every Hanna management and staff member and immediately acknowledged the rumor. To everyone's surprise, I confirmed that the rumor had some truth to it! I explained that every company at some time or another will have some degree of financial difficulties and I outlined exactly what the problems were and how we were already dealing with it. I also asked each and every member of our organization to come forward with any other suggestions of how else they might believe we could overcome the problems successfully within a sixty to ninety day period. Surprisingly, there were some very good ideas, which we implemented immediately, and everyone pulled together and we overcame the problem successfully!

One aspect of the solution that I decided to implement was to contact every one of my creditors and bring the problem to their attention before my competition had the opportunity to do so. The result was extraordinarily fantastic for Hanna. In fact many creditors extended additional credit even though we were already behind in some of our payments. They saw our honesty in communicating both the problems we were experiencing and the solutions that were being implemented to be commendable! Obviously, had I chosen to be secretive and ignore the rumor... who knows what may have happened. Instead, I used the power of communication to strengthen our organization and team spirit.

Rumors may be true or false, but the negative power of such forces can be dangerous if not handled appropriately and in a comprehensive manner. You should always be sensitive and fair when hearing gossip that may or may not be the truth about a company. Do not be like most people and simply chime in. Do not contribute to gossip that you have not confirmed to be true. This can be damaging not only to the company for which you work, but it can be damaging to you personally.

LIES

I have always felt that if a person would lie to me they would more than likely also steal from me. I have always invited my employees to share the truth with me in exchange for leniency and possible forgiveness. If I had to discover that they lied to me I would have far less compassion and it would usually lead to instant dismissal. I believe that we all have the capacity for being somewhat dishonest, especially if we can justify it in our minds. Everyone has a different idea of what they believe is dishonesty. Since this can range from a person eating a candy bar without paying for it.... all the way to robbing a truck of all its cash and products, there is quite a bit of interpretation involved for the perpetrator. I always carefully and tactfully approached employees whom I had suspected of stealing products or money. When I asked them to genuinely share with me whatever they had done and that I was willing to forgive them if they shared everything with me, I would always be surprised at the results.

During my very early years in vending, I once approached an employee who had severe shortages on his route. He immediately admitted that he started taking drugs after starting to work at my company and he became caught up in the trap of financial need to support the habit. He broke down and begged me to help him overcome the problem and save his job, marriage and his life. At first I was very upset, and was about to fire him on the spot. Then I was overwhelmed with compassion. The individual offered to resign immediately. He was surprised to learn of my instinctive and immediate decision to send him in for drug consultation and rehabilitation. I offered to pay for the entire ordeal. He also decided to tell his wife of the serious offense he had committed. I promised to give him one more chance to prove his loyalty and honesty to me while he remained on probation. He proved to be one of my best employees and actually inspired me to implement our stringent drug policy, which has been enforced ever since. He worked for me for many years after that incident until he decided to take a job driving a trailer across the country for a higher salary. He had almost perfect money reports monthly and helped me implement additional strategies to prevent temptation for theft on the job. I believe that this incident made me more conscious about the severe dangers that lies can cause in the work place. This is also true when you are dealing with creditors, customers, family and friends. Sometimes it is costly to tell the truth but the benefits far outweigh the negatives. You will sometimes be exposed to a customer who claims that they lost a quarter in your machine. Do not immediately assume that they are lying even though there may be a distinct possibility that they may be lying. Be respectful of the customer, and unless you are 100% positive that they are lying to you, promptly and cheerfully make the refund. Fortunately, there are more honest people out there than not!

JEALOUSY & GREED

When you decide to go into business for yourself, beware of such behavior from others. I grew up in an affluent family and was exposed to jealousy and envy from my schoolmates, some family members, friends and others from a very early age. I was not aware of their jealousy at first because I did not understand the true meaning of such behavior. However once I began to comprehend the actions and the consequences of such behavior I was changed forever. I realized that even some of those whom I had thought were my best and closest friends, would usually be the most jealous of who they thought I was and what they thought I had. Later, I would downplay any personal accomplishments just to avoid further bouts of jealously and envy from them. Soon, I would feel the need to help these friends, family members, employees and neighbors both emotionally and financially and also down play the success of our family owned business.

As I matured and traveled the world, I discovered that there would always be a handful of family, friends and business associates who would display varying degrees of hidden or open jealousy and envy toward me. They would talk about greed of business people and the wealthy, and accuse me personally or my family of being that way. They even made fun of my spiritual growth reminding me "You can't take your wealth with you when you die". This angered me tremendously and I found myself often being placed in a position of defending my self, my beliefs and my entire family. Since all did not usually share this behavior, I learned to appreciate and respect those who treated me fairly and who accepted me for who I was and never made me feel unwelcome or unworthy of their friendship. I learned another valuable lesson from exposure to such behavior from some people. I am now convinced that the jealously and greed that these individuals actually store up inside themselves, is the cause for more pain and agony to themselves than it is to those on whom they direct such feeling! Whatever you do, never try to justify or make excuses for your personal and business success to anyone. On the other hand, never flaunt your success either! Always earn and take what you know you deserve and be generous with your time, profits and your love. There is nothing uglier than greed...not even jealousy and envy! If you are climbing the corporate ladder in a company for which you are working, also try to remember that the jealousy and greed factors are very much alive and well! If you decide to start your own company, it will be even greater! Here is a summary of my feelings regarding this matter:

"For where envying and strife is, there is confusion and every evil work" Romans 16:17

AVOID CRITICS

I would like to remind you that you should never allow critics to totally discourage and/or depress you. You can sometimes learn from critics. You should be able to reflect momentarily on their comments and take whatever portion of the comment that you feel has a shred of validity and try to learn from the comments in an objective manner without allowing it to hurt your personal feelings.

You should also remember that critics are usually disillusioned, unfocused and disappointed people who are also not as daring and optimistic as you may be. They are frequently considered to be spectators, not players.

FOOLS

Both wise people and others who are not so wise have commented over the past thousands of years that we may possibly learn something from a fool. While this may have some truth it, you should also remember to take heed from other wise and truthful sayings such as:

"Go from the presence of a foolish man, when thou perceiveth not in him the lips of knowledge" Proverbs 14:7

COST OF LOSING AN EMPLOYEE

I am always flabbergasted at the attitude of some business owners who have no idea how expensive it is to lose an employee who has been trained and is capable of generating an income for the company. Instead of making every effort to keep good employees, some managers routinely replace them in order to sometimes save a few dollars per month. They start a new employee at an entry-level salary. The truth of the matter is that when you lose an employee it will cost you several times over to train a new one, not to mention the loss of productivity and errors caused by these new employees.

BELIEVE IN YOUR PRODUCT

You cannot sell anything successfully if you do not believe in what you are selling. You must learn to understand and appreciate the unique products and services that you are presenting to others. Never try to sell a lie! Become comfortable with your offering and if you cannot present it honestly and whole-heartedly just forget it! This may seem crude. I can assure you that you will never be satisfied with yourself if you forced a sale on someone who trusted you. They in turn will eventually recognize the sorry person you truly are once they discover the deceit you portrayed. I could write volumes on this topic but I am hoping that you already recognize the importance of what I am explaining to you and that you will practice this aspect of your comprehension in order to please both yourself and your customer successfully!

Whether you choose to work for a vending company, work your way up the ladder of success or simply start your own vending company and grow it successfully, there are some basic common sense and important traits that you must learn to cultivate toward your employees, customers, management and creditors. I have selected and summarized in the following chapter some of these traits for your consideration and also for you to practice. I hope you will remember them and also find them as helpful as I have. These traits will make you a better person and a superior business manager.

Chapter 15

SOME IMPORTANT TRAITS TO REMEMBER

There are some basic traits that you should strive to adopt into your personal and business lifestyle, effective immediately, if you are not already doing so. These simple traits should be applied regardless of the business or job you decide to pursue. They are obviously not traits limited to vending business owners.

SMILE

It costs you nothing to smile at everyone with whom you come in contact. Besides, smiles are priceless and contagious too! :) The fact is that you use less facial muscles to smile than you do to frown.

WORK SMART

Find out exactly what the end result is to be and make every effort to think it through completely before jumping in and working twice as hard to accomplish very little. Plan your day, make your "to do" list of those items you really want to get done.

BE APPRECIATIVE

Remember to say "thank you" "yes sir" "yes madam" and write "thank you" notes. Let people know how much you appreciate whatever little thing they do for you. Do not take anyone or anything for granted.

BE COMPASSIONATE

Be sympathetic and caring toward all people with whom you

come in contact, especially when you know in your heart that it is appropriate to do so. Help those in need when you are able.

COURAGE

Be strong, make your plans and stick to them. Do not fall apart when someone challenges your ideas or decisions. You must remain courageous even in the face of the unknown. Being decisive is less stressful than floundering and never making a decision. It is better to make a decision than not. Regardless if the decision is right or wrong. Sometimes, consciously making no decision is very much equivalent to making a decision. This way your decision would be to wait. Listen to what others have to say politely but stick to your guns if you are not absolutely convinced that you should change your mind. Study the pros and cons and then firmly take your position. For some people, it takes courage to merely face a new day. Courage is not reserved only for the soldier on the front line of battle. Be brave and trust your instincts and soon you will be winning the battle against doubt!

SPIRITUALITY

Regardless of your religious affiliation, there is a basic divinity that is inherent within you and me at all times. If you have not discovered the awesome power, peace and beauty of this incredible gift from God... you will be forever poor... regardless of all the riches you may accumulate! Give thanks for every breath you take and be at peace with yourself. Practice what you know is spiritually sound.

PLAY

Whatever you do for a living, try to find the time to spend some of your energy on things that are non-work related. For some people that may be playing golf, playing a musical instrument or listening to music, watching a movie, reading, walking, meditating, travel or a million other playful possibilities.

EDUCATE YOURSELF

Education never ends. Whether you have no education whatsoever, a high school certificate, college degree or Doctorate Degree, it is never enough. You should always try to learn something new every day. This is the only way you can truly grow.

BE HEALTHY

Eat, sleep and exercise in a manner that is consistent with a sound body and mind. Without good health, there is hardly a need to pursue wealth because you will never enjoy it! Your body needs approximately ninety vitamins, minerals and trace elements. For every moment you are not absorbing these nutrients, a little bit of you is dying slowly. Educate yourself and make sure that you treat your body like the temple that it truly is. Most people believe that because they take a handful of vitamins they are doing well. Nothing could be further from the truth. I enjoy sharing the details I have learned over the years regarding these simple yet critical matters and am always ready, willing and able to share free information about such matters with anyone who asks. Nothing is more important than feeding your body exactly what it needs to function in peak operating condition. Most important, it makes the mind sharp and alert.

BE CALM

A temper does more damage to you than the ill feelings you are directing at others. Take a deep breath at least five or ten times whenever you feel the pangs of anger creeping up on you. You cannot make sound decisions or judgments when you are angry.

SET GOALS

You can never reach your full potential if you do not set goals. Be sure to write down your goals on paper and review then frequently.

Plan to act... then act on your plan! Once you have committed your goals to paper revise and alter them accordingly as time goes by. Here are a few words from the wise for you to ponder:

"The wisdom of the prudent is to understand his way" Proverb 14:8

"For which of you intending to build a tower, sitteth down first, and counteth the cost, whether he have sufficient to finish?" Luke 14:28

BE PERSISTENT

Work diligently toward your short term and long-term goals. Whatever you do...never...ever give up! Too many people give up just before a major break through would have happened. It is usually others who will influence your decision to quit, refuse such temptation.

MENTORS

Seek out at least one mentor from whom you may learn and emulate the ideals of your personal and business goals. Meet with them or listen to them as often as you can or as often as they will invite you to do so.

HONESTY, INTEGRITY AND CREDIBILITY

These traits cannot be borrowed, bought or stolen. You should strive to exercise these most important traits in your every day activities to the best of your ability. You will sometimes be faced with managers and staff members in organizations who have no concept of such important matters. If you recognize the frequent occurrence of such shortcomings it may be time for you to re evaluate your decision to be with that company. If such is the case, you may find it most satisfying to move on to another company or even better, build your own!

DISCRIMINATION

In my opinion, women are frequently overlooked as excellent entrepreneurs, middle and upper managers and employees in general. When given the genuine opportunities to excel, they will usually soar and make organizations operate with a higher degree of compassion, sensitivity, warmth and balance. Regardless of your gender, you should never tolerate discrimination of any kind, especially when it is against women. Did I mention that women make some of the very best vending route drivers?

There are numerous types of discrimination practices that are still very much alive and well in America and all over the world. Whenever you become conscious of such behavior, either within your heart or from those around you make a genuine effort to stop and remember that the divine presence that is found within you...also dwells within each and every other person...even if they look and sound different to you!

DARE TO BE DIFFERENT

You are a unique being. There is no one else just like you.

Therefore never be satisfied to follow the same old routine that everyone else may have deemed ordinary and acceptable. Think seriously and when appropriate, playfully, when evaluating everything that is presented to you, and do so independently and creatively!

PERFECTION

Regardless how hard you try to be perfect for others, you will no doubt fall short of this goal! Do not be disappointed or discouraged when you do not accomplish all that you set out to do! Remember that you are only human and it is perfectly ok to appear to be less than perfect! Love yourself first, because until you do...you will not have the capacity to love anyone else or to know and appreciate the perfection of the almighty God who orchestrates the universe with such precise perfection and grace. That perfection is always within you!

BE POSITIVE

Avoid those people who are always telling you that it is not possible to accomplish your goals and dreams! This is a very contagious illness that you want to stay clear of at all costs. You would not consciously kiss someone with strep throat...unless you are anxious to join him or her in their suffering. Hundreds of books have been written on the power of a positive mind...read a few of them if you believe that you may possibly need an attitude adjustment. The fact that you are already reading this book is a strong indication that you are already moving in the right direction!

POLITE & THOUGHTFUL

It does not cost you anything to be polite and thoughtful. This does not have to be anything more than an acknowledging smile, or lending a sympathetic ear to a family member, friend, neighbor, employee or member of management. Send a thank you note for small gestures of kindness others have shown you. Remember to say "Thank you" and "Please" and other such polite words of acknowledgment and respect. Take time to listen. Don't rush anyone who is communicating with you, especially when the communication is of a personal and sensitive kind. Your customers will appreciate you beyond your expectations when you show such simple and basic courtesies.

HIRING EMPLOYEES

Once you have decided to hire an employee, treat them exactly how you would want to be treated if you were going to do the same job. Pay them fairly and if possible, exceed the market salary expectations. This behavior will pay great dividends. Take a chance on those who may have a handicap, which will not affect the job for which they are to perform. Treat them with great respect during the interviewing process and continue the same respectful attitude with them in the future whether they are hired or not. truthful and thorough with prospective employees. Do not attempt to lure them away from their existing jobs with unrealistic promises. If hired, these will be your most important assets. The level of respect you shared with them will mirror their level of respect for you!

CONCLUSION

Now that you have read this book, you should have a much better idea of the basics of vending and what you might want to do and what you might want to avoid. Vending is a very lucrative business and you can indeed make a fortune if you do it correctly. I have shared some of my personal philosophy about life, work and passion in the hope that you will find some of these traits helpful on your road to success.

It is helpful to have some legal and accounting assistance to insure that you are structured properly for the maximum security and return on investment if you are setting up your own vending business. Practice the strategies mentioned in this book and you will be on your way to building a successful vending operation. Whether you buy new, used or refurbished vending equipment or manual, electronic or electro mechanical equipment, you now have a head start on the facts concerning each of these types of equipment.

You can count on me personally to be here for you should you have questions or if you should need consultation at a more advanced level. Since I had started my own vending business from one vending machine and built it into a multi million-dollar organization, I understand all the angles that you may possibly need to know. Vending is not a "get rich quick" business. It is a solid labor-intensive cash business that is in great demand, especially if you give excellent service.

Now you must start planning your next step. It is important to ask yourself: What type of vending equipment appeals to me? How large a business do I want to grow? How much capital do I have? How much capital will I need to borrow? Within what radius of miles from home do I wish to operate? What will my flyer promote? Will I be able to operate with my existing vehicle? Is my apartment or home garage large enough to house my operation?

Will I need a locator or will I start out small and handle my own sales? Will I work for a vending company before owning my own company? Would I prefer to work permanently for a vending company instead of owning a company at this point in my life? If I should decide to work for a vending company, in what area or position do I believe I may be the most effective? Will I need to keep my job while starting up my new business? Should I incorporate my spouse and/or my children in my business? Should I buy an existing vending business or buy equipment and place them on my own?

I wish you every success in the world and look forward to hearing from you in the future. I encourage you to communicate any information that you believe I should expand upon in future updates to this book, future Hanna audio cassette tapes, video tapes, catalogs and news letters. I may also consider preparing a package of sample forms and drafts of possible communications that may be used in your vending business if you believe that these may be helpful.

I wish you God's richest blessings and all the personal, business and spiritual prosperity in the world!

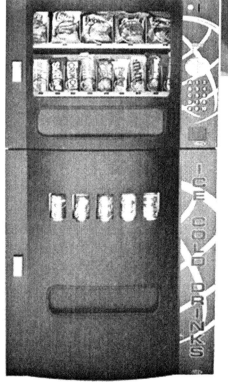

NOTES

ABOUT THE AUTHOR

Charles Hanna was unemployed and practically broke upon arrival to America in 1975. He was sitting by the pool at his apartment complex one day reviewing the "help wanted" ads while his friends were discussing whose turn it was to go to the grocery store to buy potato chips to compliment the cold beverages they drank on those hot summer days. During the conversation, one of his friends suggested that a person could become wealthy if they would place a vending machine in the clubhouse. Charles, having an entrepreneurial background, was determined to give this idea a try. He immediately got up and walked into the apartment complex manager's office and proposed placing a snack vending machine for the residents. When the manager saw the need and agreed with very little resistance, Charles was astonished. He could hardly afford his next meal but was overjoyed at the thought of starting his new business. The rest is history.

Charles went on to build one of the largest vending companies in the Kansas City area and a "one of a kind" vending organization in the world. The *full service vending division* grew rapidly and was later followed by an *equipment sales division, wholesale distribution of products, snack shops, cafeteria operations, and consultations on vending machine scams* and also the publishing of *The World's 1st Vending Machine Price Catalog*. Charles has always been passionate about educating small and large vendors about vending machine scams because he was a victim of a few vending scams himself when he first started out in vending in the mid 1970's. He established himself as the source for free information regarding vending machine scams, hundreds of phone calls were being directed at Hanna regarding assistance on vending and related scams. Toward the end of the millennium 2000, Charles and Michael decided that it was time to focus on specific new personal goals in their lives and they decided to sell one of their divisions, the local *full service vending division* to another family owned vending organization in Missouri. They concluded their transaction, they both decided to build their own individual organizations whereby they could grow into areas that best suited their individual strengths. Therefore, the merger of their local *full service vending division* ended a 25-year-old successful partnership. Charles agreed to stay for a limited time and assist the organization that bought his full service vending division in order to insure a smooth transition and until the organization no longer would need his services.

Charles continues to promote The World's 1st Vending Machine Price Catalog and ships vending machines to customers all over the world, provide consultation on vending matters and also shares sources on basic tax strategies and credit repair and other important investment and related business activities. He shares all that he has learned about nutrition and the positive impact such actions can have on one's personal and business life.

Charles served as president of his local Rotary Club and he has been recognized over the years for his extremely heavy involvement in numerous organizations including his local Chamber of Commerce where he served on the board of directors and also received a Life-Time Member status among many other awards. He has been involved in numerous vending industry related organizations and civic activities over the years and consulted with some of the largest vending organizations in the world. He also consulted with government entities and business organizations in the USA and internationally regarding their need for assistance in all vending and related matters.

Born on the island of Jamaica in the capital of Kingston in 1952, he was raised by affluent business Lebanese parents,

Habib and Victoria Hanna. He was the third child of a total of four children from that marriage (Rene, Janet, Charles and Michael). His parents were extremely industrious and successful business people internationally. He attended private schools in both Lebanon and Jamaica. He studied some Spanish, Latin and French but was encouraged to learn Arabic, and most important, he would perfect his primary language, English. Jamaica was a British Colony and so proper "English" was the order of the day! Today he is still fluent in a Lebanese dialect of Arabic and proper English, not to mention a fluent Jamaican Patois. He is always enrolled in some form of continuing education programs and encourages everyone around him to do the same.

In his early years, Charles made long trips to Beirut, Lebanon. His parents wanted him to visit the "old country" and that was how he learned the Arabic language. He found himself being taught Arabic and French for the few years he attended school before returning to Jamaica. Charles and his younger brother Michael were always together and were also best of friends. Even though he was born and raised in a Christian family, he learned to appreciate and respect the religious beliefs of his many friends who were Muslims, Christians, Buddhists, Hindus and other faiths. He found it fascinating to interact with Princes and Princesses and many other members of royal families from all over the world. For the next 10 to 15 years of his early life he traveled back and forth from Jamaica and Lebanon and studied at the best private boarding schools in Lebanon and Jamaica. Charles loved music and started a band, which became successful in Jamaica and later led to the composing, recording and distribution of several records and numerous TV appearances. Although Charles was only a teenager and not an accomplished musician, he loved the music business and the excitement of the music and entertainment industry.

In the early 1970's there was much political unrest on the island of Jamaica and during one of the turbulent times he experienced what he thought, had to be the nightmare of his life. Their "family owned" factories and other business operations were destroyed in a major fire that devastated the family and almost all of their assets were lost. Charles, who never completed high school, decided to accept a friend's invitation to visit America and attend college while his parents struggled with their financial dilemma. He excelled in his studies and later graduated with honors and decided to return to Beirut where his family still had some business assets. He had successfully assisted in managing his family assets in Beirut from a very young age. However no sooner than he arrived in Beirut after the completion of his college studies in the USA, the civil war broke out in Beirut and he was trapped in Lebanon for the following two years. He later successfully escaped from the civil war in Beirut. It was only then, realizing that almost everything else that the family had owned was lost; he decided to return to make America his home. He would soon marry the girl he dated in college, Linda Abrajano.

To most foreigners, America is the land of opportunity. He had learned to negotiate in life and death matters and was exposed to the worst nightmare of his life during the Civil war. He watched as one of the most beautiful countries in the world was reduced to rubble. At every opportunity in his current interactions, Charles reminds Americans how fortunate they are to wake up in America every day. He expresses his sincere pride in being an American and never forgets such a distinct honor and privilege.

Charles continues to live an exciting, fulfilling and fast paced life of adventure and challenges and is always alert to new and exciting business opportunities. He is health conscious and became an avid vegetarian (vegan) in the late 80's and remains committed to this healthy way of life. He has always promoted a choice of healthy products in vending machines long before it was the trendy thing to do. He strongly pursues the development of his spiritual and very healthy, positive approach to life.

He practices meditation and Yoga with a fun attitude while maintaining the fundamental Christian traits with which he was raised. He also believes in securing personal and business financial success for himself and his loved ones and is always willing to share wholeheartedly with others how they may do the same. He adores his two daughters, Tiffany and Krystal. They both are active teenagers who share much of their dad's enthusiasm for life and are ever willing to learn and participate in the family business while incorporating their very hectic teenage schedules of school, friendships, jobs, career planning, hobbies and traveling when possible.

Charles continually enrolls in business and personal seminars, college courses, meditation retreats and other similar activities. He freely shares whatever he learns with others who have a desire to know more. He has offered consultation to all who requested it for the past 26 years. He has communicated with more than 25,000 contacts, which are logged, into his data base and he intends to continue consulting with interested parties well into the new millennium.

His purpose for writing this book was to educate interested individuals, established vending machine operators, manufacturers, entrepreneurs, food and beverage distributors, government agents at every level, the media, lawyers, and a vast array of people who may have an interest in the vending industry. Most important, he wants to help prevent vending scams nationally and internationally as much as possible.

SOME FUN AND IMPORTANT DETAILS ABOUT VENDING MACHINES!

Every 15 minutes, more than 3.5 million coins are inserted in vending machines located in the USA. That translates into approximately 12.5 million coins every hour. Because vending machines do not take vacations, this goes on 24 hours per day, 365 days per year!

During the 1980's more than approximately five billion cups of hot beverages and eight billion confections and snacks sold through vending machines annually. At that time the total annual vended sales volume was at approximately $17 billion. That was about $70 per capita.

By the mid 1990's, the total annual vended sales volume had reached approximately 30 BILLION dollars! Do Americans like vending machines or what? :) 2000 and beyond promises to be only bigger and better.........

Charles Hanna's story was featured in
<u>Success Magazine</u>, August 1988.